Abner's Curse:

A Diary of Essays
from a Baseball Itinerant

Tommy Szarka

PublishAmerica
Baltimore

First printing

At the specific preference of the author, PublishAmerica allowed
this work to remain exactly as the author intended, verbatim, without
editorial input.

ISBN: 1-4241-6984-4
PUBLISHED BY PUBLISHAMERICA, LLLP
www.publishamerica.com
Baltimore

Printed in the United States of America

Author's Note: This book describes the author's experiences while watching baseball games across the country during 2006. The author recorded these events immediately after (or while) the incidents occurred with meticulous note taking to ensure accuracy. However, some names and identifying details of numerous individuals have been omitted or altered for privacy.

Acknowledgments

I would like to thank anyone who went to a game with me during the 2006 season. In alphabetical order: Tim Barcomb, Andrea Barton, Mike Barton, Katie Benson, James Bradley, Tommy Case, Tyler Coffin, Suzie Ellsworth, Steve Ezzo, Tim Freer, Erika Fritjofson, Ryan Gramaglia, Bryan Harmer, Hillary Haynes, Laura Hays, Jim Kane, Todd Kirkey, Mark Kulka, Scott Lacombe, Gary Mikel, Matt Perry, Tony Perry, Avrum Pesner, Mike Pitts, Kate Quint, Elizabeth Schultheis, Chris Szarka, and Tom Szarka. Additionally, I would like to thank the following people that attended games with me prior to this season, but were unable to join me this year. In alphabetical order: Mark Anderson, Brandon Barcomb, Emily Case, Amanda Crowley, Jason Culverhouse, Lindsey Ellsworth, Christina Freer, Jen Gafford, Dan Girard, Jason Lammers, Tim Lennon, Laura Mandell, Ann Parks, Jack Phillips, Zach Richardson, Shannon Staples, Dave Steele, and Evan Weaver. Also thanks for the continued support from the following people: Melissa Szarka, Lisa Szarka, Margaret Mere, Matt Capell, Becky Worthington, Sarah Kenney, and Ashley Janisewski. There are others, too, but the line needed to be cut somewhere. Lastly, in addition to those that made it to games with me, there are countless others that increased my enjoyment at numerous ballparks, but I never got the chance to find out everyone's name. Thanks to all.

Table of Contents

Foreword—
The Essence of
Human Existence

Wherever I go, people ask me why I like baseball so much. I could cloud the answer by saying, like so many other poetic writers and sport aficionados, that I adore how it combines symmetry and simplicity with chaos, explosiveness and complexity; how hundreds of possibilities can come from any pitch, thousands with every batter and countless millions in every game. Every game, whether it is played at a dilapidated sandlot or in an expertly manicured major league cathedral, employs flawed players making mistakes, making adjustments to those mistakes for future success, and then continuing a cycle of metamorphosis to combat failure in some sort of Darwinian Theory of survival of the fittest. It perfectly embodies the essence of human existence. If that doesn't make someone sorry they asked the question, I don't know what would.

The shorter reason for why I love the game of baseball is because it's fun. No other game combines all sorts of athletic activities in one sport. Hand-eye coordination, speed, arm strength, core strength, quick reactions and intellectual intuitiveness are imperative qualities for the game to be played well. Yet, if a player excels so tremendously in one general area, imperfect players can attain immortal status, a fact that can be attested to by the Baseball Hall of

Fame's members who couldn't read or write, who were overweight, or who were half blind. The game simply allows for dreamers, including both wannabe players and its fandom. When I was young, I included myself in the former, but now as a washed up former pseudo athlete who topped out at 77 miles per hour off the mound, I gladly count myself in the latter.

Handicapped by a modest budget, a cramped schedule and held hostage by the whims of grateful-to-have-me hosts, I have made the most of my baseball dreams by visiting 50 professional ballparks and attending 250 professional baseball games since the start of the 2003 season. Some would consider this excessive while others would be unimpressed. For those that think it overindulgent, understand that I'm not the average baseball fan and that I live for watching games, no matter the level of competition. For those that feel 250 games over a four-year span and 50 parks aren't that many, I would point out that the closest major or minor league ballpark for me is a 150-mile round trip, and that one is located in an entirely different country. Any ballpark located in the United States is, at minimum, a 280-mile round trip, and with gasoline at its current level, the petrol prices make every ballgame I attend cost a minimum of $40 before I even take a bite from a hot dog. That also doesn't include hotels, airline tickets or other bulkier costs, and I'm not rich, so do the math.

I'm not complaining. I love baseball and the costs that surround the game are a fair price to pay for me to see the top professionals play their game. In seeing these games I've met a variety of people that also find themselves at home while at the ballpark. Some are wonderfully wacky, others are clever and friendly, while others are whipped into some sort of nonsensical frenzy that I can hardly comprehend. But I like to try.

That's what this book is about. It's not just about a person who likes going to ballgames all over the country. It's also about the people in the stands and those on the field. In these pages you will find both first-person and third-person accounts about some really odd fans, anecdotes about soon-to-be well-known ballplayers and some never-to-be well-known ballplayers, tales of life on the road in the eastern United States, and stories from the author's past, a guy many will never have met. By the end, maybe you will want to know more about me, or perhaps you will want to contribute to the Cory Patton fund (see South Bend, Indiana, in mid-June). After a tease like that, how could anyone not want to continue forward?

Most of the stories are separate from one another and are written in a loose diary format, but the tales from each game also hold to a form of essay as well, jumping back and forth from baseball and the trials and tribulations of real life for the fans and the ballplayers on the field. In addition to the stories that were written, there were numerous fascinating discoveries that I simply did not have the energy or inclination to expound upon. These include the kindness of the Pittsburgh Public School system courteously providing metal detectors prior to the Futures Game (a troublesome thought), what appeared to be a full-size plastic blow up doll in the bullpen at Joe Bruno Stadium (a groupie?), a player in Connecticut requiring a restraining order against an overzealous season-ticket holder (after meeting her, I would have considered a barbed wire fence as well), a near fistfight between teammates Reid Engel and Luis Exposito of the Lowell Spinners (after a 13-2 win in Vermont), and a senior citizen proudly proclaiming "I'm addicted to baseball just like every other man in America. Well, the straight ones anyway." Not every game lent itself to a detailed account, despite such wonderful nuggets in the previous lines, so I had to pick and choose which games would merit inclusion in the upcoming pages. I hope that I chose wisely and that everyone will enjoy *Abner's Curse*.

Dusting Off the Cobwebs in Spring Training

For those who have only attended regular season baseball games, spring training is really a totally different experience. Regulars might get three at bats in a game and are usually gone by the fifth inning, replaced by players who are sometimes years away from the big leagues or by retreads trying to earn any kind of spot in the organization. It is a time for some to kick off the rust of a long off-season and regain their timing, and for others it is a time to show that they can still play professional ball.

I started off the 2006 season with a game between two Fort Myers teams, the Minnesota Twins and Boston Red Sox, on March 12th. I almost didn't get to go because of the Clarkson University baseball schedule. Unless you are Tom Clancy, John Grisham or someone of that ilk, it isn't particularly easy to make a living as a writer, especially if you only produce one baseball book every five years like I seem to be doing in my brief writing career. Therefore, I've supplemented my income by working as a sports information and media director at this New York institution, just 20 miles from the United States-Canadian border. Fortunately, a significant perk is the annual trip to Florida for the first quarter of the college team's schedule. It's hard to convince people that when I travel to Florida in March, it's not for spring break, but to work. Everyone believes that the coaching staff and I go out to bars every night and just play a game during the day, then merrily go back to the hotel bar to get ripped, which is exactly the opposite of what happens. Preparation for any game is lengthy and most of the day is spent trying to make sure nothing goes wrong, on or off the field, with a bunch of college kids. We're usually asleep by 10 p.m. The college's schedule wasn't kind to me in 2005 and I didn't attend a spring training game that year, but I was able to slide one game in for 2006 after reviewing the early returns from the schedule-makers. I purchased advance tickets for the game between the two Fort Myers cross town rivals.

City of Palms Park, the spring home of the Boston Red Sox, was completed in 1992 and is reminiscent of a minor league ballpark with a seating capacity of a little under 7,000. It's a nice yard and is sold out for virtually ever game with only standing room tickets available, mirroring the difficulty of acquiring tickets at Fenway Park. The great thing about spring training is that with a smaller crowd you can get closer to the field and to the players, allowing for better interaction as if you were at a minor league game. Red Sox legend Johnny Pesky, one of only three players in baseball history to record 200 hits in his first three major league seasons, was sitting in a lawn chair on the third base side and was signing autographs for kids and adults alike. The grouping of autograph hunters was significant, but one could tell he does this all the time. Most people, myself not included, were prepared for Pesky to be there and had all kinds of Pesky stuff ready for him to affix his signature. The best piece of memorabilia was the David Halberstam book "The Teammates," a book about four Red Sox members (Ted Williams, Dom Dimaggio, Bobby Doerr and Pesky) from the 1940s and 1950s.

After about ten minutes of standing on the wall on the first base side, I decided that I would have Pesky sign my ticket stub. It took about three minutes of waiting and a security guard grabbed my ticket stub and handed it to Pesky, who took his time to make his autograph legible. It's too bad Pesky isn't constantly surrounded by those security guards to protect his frail frame. A few days later he was hit by a line drive during a college game played at the park and it broke his leg. He made it out of the ordeal fine, but he is such a goodwill ambassador to the team and to the sport, it wouldn't surprise me if the team placed him in a kind of bulletproof plastic bubble in 2007.

The game started and the three Clarkson coaches and I stood along the wall between the first and second decks of the stadium, our standing-room spots. It was uncomfortable to be on our feet in the 85-degree heat for the first hour or so, but our lack of comfort paled in comparison to that of Jonathan Papelbon, who started the game for the Red Sox. He struggled mightily with his control in the first few innings. I know the Red Sox like him as a starter, but he might prove to be a better fit in the bullpen where he spent most of his time in the majors last year as a late-season call up.* Keith Foulke is far from a sure thing and Craig Hansen isn't ready to pitch in the majors just yet, so maybe Papelbon can be a set-up man or part-time closer, finishing with maybe 30 holds and 10 to 15 saves as a break for Foulke.

As the game moved on through the first few innings, you could really hear the conversations start rolling. I find that in the first inning or two of a game that everyone is really into the action on the field, but it isn't until the third or fourth when the batting orders start to turn over that fans begin commenting on players of the present and past.

A couple of old-timers to my left were having a fairly informed discussion. In overhearing them (or eavesdropping, if you wish), they had discussed the origination of the term Texas Leaguer and the umpiring mechanics of the infield fly rule. The two went back and forth on the infield fly discussion with good reason. Boston's Enrique Wilson drifted out of the infield on a pop fly hit by the Twins' Tony Batista with one out in the inning and runners on first and second. The ball was sky high and Wilson ended up in shallow right field to make the catch. The infield fly signal was made late by the umpire, but it was certainly the right call. The two debated the point enthusiastically for a half inning before something new caught their attention. That something, or rather someone, was the much-traveled Ruben Sierra.

---

* *I would like to mention, because I know some wouldn't believe me, that I did in fact write this before Papelbon was moved in to the closer's role in Boston, where he has been wildly successful in his first full season.*

"I say he is 40," one said to the other after some moderate, yet jovial, discussion of Sierra's impending social security status. "Mmm, I think he's 41 or 42," the second said. "Probably 41." I couldn't help but chime in. I always try to end these arguments with facts instead of unfounded conjecture. "Are you talking about Sierra?" I asked. The two both indicated I was on the right track. "He was born in November of 1965." "So he's 41," one said. "No, he's 40," the other responded. "Eh, let's call it even and say he's 40 and a half," I said. The two men laughed and followed up with another question.

"You seem to know a lot about the Twins. Did Santana come up through the system?"

"Johan Santana was a Rule 5 pick a ways back," I replied. "He actually signed with the Astros originally, but he didn't spend any time in the minors with the Twins." I decided not to explain the Rule 5 pick to these guys. With all of Santana's success in the last few years, if they were unaware that he didn't originally start with the Twins, then they likely were unfamiliar with the Rule 5 draft system that allows teams to select three- and four-year players left off the 40-man rosters of other organizations.

Despite the questioning of Santana, I was satisfied that these men were not idiots. Unfortunately, the guys to my right could not continue the trend in City of Palms Park. A group of Boston fans about my age proved to me why a little knowledge is a dangerous thing. Because that is all they possessed. Boston catcher Dusty Brown had a difficult time corralling Jonathan Papelbon's pitches and Franklyn Nunez, Papelbon's replacement, wasn't doing much better at locating his offerings in the strike zone.

"Where's Varitek?" one beer-swilling Sox fan said. "Is that Flaherty? He stinks." The others agreed that Flaherty stunk.

As I mentioned earlier, I try to answer fans' questions during games. I don't know why. It's probably my inherent desire, as some type of intellectual elitist, for order in the universe and to have everyone possess my knowledge of the game. I made an exception for these fans, for there are some that simply cannot be helped.

15

Anyone who was a baseball fan attending a game in March of 2006 would likely know that there was this thing called the World Baseball Classic going on. These life-long Sox fans (I can only assume; they had the jerseys and the accents) forgot that Jason Varitek was off catching for the USA team in the WBC. He even hit a grand slam against Canada only a few days earlier. Apparently the 400-foot bomb he hit to left center on national television which was reported repeatedly on every national sports news service had escaped them. On a less severe note, John Flaherty had retired five days earlier. Again, these guys certainly had their collective fingers on the pulse. I decided to listen a little longer until they made me nauseated. Maybe I have some kind of social anxiety disorder with symptoms brought to the surface by stupidity surrounding me.

"They say Toronto is going to be a team to beat this year," one said to another. "They signed a couple guys and signed, uh, the closer, uh, Wagner."

I could have sworn Billy Wagner had signed with the New York Mets, but perhaps I had been misinformed. It took me close to a second to remove the furrow from my brow when I realized that I was right, Billy Wagner was with the Mets and BJ Ryan, formerly of the Orioles, had signed with the Blue Jays. I know it seems ridiculous that something as simple as confusion over a pair of relievers would send a sickening feeling throughout my body, but it is this type of fan that calls in to those pathetic sports talk shows on the radio where the two combatants then battle to see who can yell louder.

Luckily, I wouldn't need to test my body's annoyance endurance any longer. Like a beacon in the night, one of the Clarkson player's parents passed us along that cluttered wall and offered us his seats behind the plate for the final four innings of the game since he was departing the game for another engagement. We gladly accepted and my stomach settled down in the shade.

All in all, it was a fine day at the park. I collected a few autographs of some Minnesota fringe players in addition to Red Sox legend Johnny Pesky. There was only one problem: I needed more. I had come to Florida with only one ticket, but this one game was not going to be enough to give me my fix of pro baseball.

As luck would have it, one game turned into three during the week. The following day I went back to City of Palms Park for another afternoon game, and then followed that up two days later with a hastily planned journey across town to see the Pittsburgh Pirates take on Minnesota Twins.

While City of Palms Park is almost in downtown Fort Myers, Hammond Stadium is about six miles out of the city/commercial strip. It is a beautiful stadium, complete with a man-made waterfall in front, and the park is surrounded by other baseball facilities in the Lee County Sports Complex. Boston's park is purely for spring training, but Hammond Stadium is also the home of the Florida State League's Fort Myers Miracle, the Class A affiliate of the Twins. What seems like a half-mile sidewalk leads up to the ballpark entrance, and the parking area around it is filled with street signs of former Minnesota greats, a simplistic and transparent touch. The Twins have been at the site for 16 years and the Miracle have been affiliated with Minnesota since 1993, so it's not like Rod Carew, Harmon Killebrew, Jim Kaat or Tony Oliva spent a lot of time in Fort Myers toiling in the minor leagues. In fact, the Twins (or Washington Senators prior to moving to Minnesota) spent nearly half a century in Orlando before embarking to Fort Myers in 1990. I think the Miracle and Twins would be better off embracing the players who have actually played there. Say, like Kirby Puckett, Torii Hunter, or even Joe Mauer. It should be pointed out, however obvious, that they did not ask me. And I doubt they will.

I smartly sat in the shade on another roasting day in the mid-afternoon sun and was left alone for the most part. A college team from Illinois sat behind me, and a few players grilled their coach about anything and everything about his days in pro ball. I learned enough about his career to figure out who he and his team was. His name was Lynn Carlson and he was a draft pick of Pittsburgh back in 1990. Carlson had a solid knowledge of the game, as one would expect, but he missed a few things about the business aspect of the game. But hey, nobody's perfect.

And it still bothers me.

Out of the corner of my eye, I saw a man making his way towards me. It happens all the time. I carry a scorebook roughly the size of a small flat screen television and it garners a great deal of attention from numerous gawkers in every ballpark. I wouldn't trade it for the world. The Ultimate Scorebook, approximately 11x17, offers just about everything anyone could ever want in a scorebook and even provides a notes section in the middle. I figured this was just another man who needed to make an unoriginal, drab comment or someone who needed to know how to notate a strikeout.

"Who is pitching for the Twins," the man asked.

"Matt Garza," I responded. Figuring he had no clue who Matt Garza was, I decided to elaborate. Though I have limited experience at spring training games, I've noticed a normal refrain in the later innings of most spring training games which goes a little something like this: "Who?" Since most of the fans aren't familiar with anyone outside the major leagues, every time there is a pinch-hitter or a relief pitcher and the crowd can't pronounce the name, a collective "who" comes from the mass of people.

So, before the guy could even ask who this Matt Garza was, I cut him off. "He was a first-round draft pick for the Twins two years ago." Almost as soon as I completed the remark, I felt that same sickening feeling in my stomach that made itself known a few days earlier listening to the Red Sox fans figure where Billy Wagner had signed. The Minnesota Twins enjoyed a veritable bonanza of first-round draft picks in 2004, picking Trevor Plouffe, Glen Perkins, Jay Rainville, Kyle Waldrop and Matt Fox in the first 60 picks or so, thanks to free-agent defections that provided the team with several compensation selections. However, Garza was not in that group. He was a first-round pick out of Fresno State in *2005*. That would be less than a year ago at the time of this game's viewing. Here I am, trying to show off how smart I am in front of this guy, Lynn Carlson, and the entire Greenville team behind me, and I provide faulty information. He didn't know my mistake as he nodded his head and returned to his seat, but I wanted to crawl under mine and hoped he had an incredibly short memory or didn't hear me.

I suppose spring training isn't just for the players.

Allentown Here We Come

Is there anything more lonely or pathetic than one person randomly batting together thunder stix in an empty stadium?

And right on cue, a pair of the plastic monstrosities bangs four times in the hopes of mounting a rally in the sixth inning. This is Ottawa in April, where crowds sometimes go unreported because of their miniscule size, a disappointing fact since the city and its suburbs constitute close to a million inhabitants. On this particular April evening, the thought of the Indianapolis Indians and the hometown Lynx so excited the locals that 250 fans (688 according to the box score report) scattered the 8,000-seat stadium and allowed each and every paying customer to hear any number of catcalls from the upper deck or every player cuss as they grounded out meekly to an infielder. If you were really close to the action, it was a joy to try to control your own gag reflex as a first baseman hocks some spit from the back of his throat and thrusts it to the infield dirt with a slight curvature of the tongue and a rush of air from his lungs.

A decade ago, Ottawa was a new city in the International League and drew impressive crowds. The city is one of Canada's largest and is the capital of the country, so one would imagine that it wouldn't be too difficult to muster crowds above a few thousand even on the coldest of spring evenings. However, the Montreal Expos affiliation was discontinued several seasons ago, ending whatever lingering interest the city had for baseball. After all, hockey is king in Canada. I was reminded of that on two separate occasions, once at the beginning of the game and again in the final outs. At the conclusion of the national anthems, a middle-aged man, who was sitting in a section all his own, shouted for officials to "drop the puck." Obviously he was joking, but two others were seemingly at the wrong venue, discussing the starting goaltenders of the Ottawa Senators and Montreal Canadiens in their battle for seeds in the upcoming Stanley Cup playoffs. One could hardly blame them, seeing how the hometown Lynx were trailing by seven runs in the ninth inning, heading towards their first loss of the young season, but when the run-differential was referred to as "points," I longed for the final out so I could watch Baseball Tonight on ESPN.

I can make fun of Ottawa, as I have become a regular there over the past three seasons. Having attended nearly 50 games at Lynx Stadium since May 2003, I've come to know many of the season-ticket holders. Those that frequent the park know the game and the organization surprisingly well. It's those that come sporadically who are somewhat of an embarrassment to the city. For instance, waiting outside just a few minutes before the doors opened to allow the growing throng of fans to enter (all 10 of us), there was one man who decided to take the time to sit down on a bench and clip his nails. A Mo Rocca look-alike (I suppose it could have been Mo Rocca, who has become quite famous for his witticisms on the numerous VH1 retrospective specials, but I didn't want to bother him) was quite polite when asking for autographs from the opposing players, but sadly mispronounced some of the players' names. Another fan was able to yell to another in the cavernous stadium and question her work ethic as she sold 50-50 tickets, which somehow raised $112 for the winner.

The stadium isn't awful, though many of the players don't appreciate it because of its overall lack of amenities, but the majority of the people are actually overly polite, which seems to be a common characteristic of many Canadians. In fact, when Indians' third baseman Jose Bautista yelled a profanity after fouling off a cock shot, a fan responded with, "Hey, hey, get him out of there," but not cruelly, more apologetically for the situation, making the fan seem embarrassed that it could have possibly happened in this ballpark.

And instead of being depressed by the score, the fans were willing to participate in one of the more nonsensical acts I've seen at a ballpark in some time. Most stadiums simply have the spectators rise and sing "Take Me Out to the Ballgame" in the seventh inning. Ottawa employs its mascot, Scratch, to lead the crowd in a sort of geriatric aerobic workout with odd flailing arm movements that could easily poke out the eye of the person sitting in the adjacent seat. It is a ridiculous thing to watch, let alone take part in, so the Lynx fans must really enjoy making the creator of these movements, which rivals the chicken dance for inanity, quite content.

The worst kept secret in minor league baseball is that the Lynx will not only change affiliates in 2007, probably joining Philadelphia, but likely will spend only one more season in Ottawa. Purchases and plans have begun in an effort to move the team, with the likely destination being Allentown, Pennsylvania, where the team would be a natural fit for the Phillies, only a hundred miles down the road. The once-proud franchise is doomed to become a member of an independent league, something for which I'm not willing to travel. I'll miss the stadium and the people, so I guess I'll just have to make the most of the next two years, as will the other 250 people braving the elements in early April.

Derek Jeter's Guardian Angel

Originally when the thought of this book had come to mind, I didn't want to revisit, in writing, the same stadiums over and over again. However, April is a busy month for me at work and longer trips were impossible. Therefore, Ottawa was visited two more times and what a shame it would be to not to record the happenings on these two occasions.

Routinely, I try to arrive to ballparks as soon as the gates are open. The tail end of batting practice can be entertaining and I also enjoy wandering about the park. Sometimes I try to get autographs of the upcoming stars or former major leaguers playing out the string. Ottawa is the best for this since no one is there. In late April, with the Charlotte Knights visiting the Lynx, there were only three people waiting outside to enter the ballpark, including myself, a Latino man who arrived via cab, and someone else I recognized from my visits to Olympic Stadium in Montreal before the team moved to Washington. I never knew his name and never wanted to know his name since it seemed his only goal in life was to make others' lives less cheerful. I once witnessed him berate a member of the Minnesota Twins pitching corps while the player was talking to relatives or friends in Montreal. It absolutely baffled me. The guy wasn't pitching, he was simply trying to have a pleasant talk before the game started. At a minor league ballpark, where you can get closer to the action and have more contact with the players, the heckler is an absolute nuisance. He is a roly-poly type, not too different than a Caucasian version of the McDonald's character Grimace. When he stood next to me by the Charlotte dugout, not only did I long for a quarter-pounder and a McFlurry, but I also quickly came to realize I was in for trouble.

The Charlotte Knights roster was stacked with prospects and older established big leaguers. After struggling in 2005 with one of the worst records in the International League, the team had started strong in 2006, winning twice as many games as it had lost. Among the prospects were Ryan Sweeney, a 21-year-old 2003 first-round draft pick, Jerry Owens, who narrowly lost Chicago's starting centerfield job to Brian Anderson, and Josh Fields, a standout football and baseball player at Oklahoma State who was picked in the first round of the 2004 draft. The veterans were also impressive, with former Los Angeles Dodgers Rookie of the Year and Pacific Rim trailblazer Hideo Nomo, minor league vagabond Ernie Young, and a former prospect that had once been dubbed "the next Mickey Mantle," Ruben Rivera. A Yankees prospect in the mid-1990s, Rivera's strike zone judgment left a lot to be desired and he never panned out the way New York had envisioned. He bounced around the minors for a while and gained a great deal of notoriety when he stole Derek Jeter's glove during spring training a few years ago to sell to a sports memorabilia dealer. When his crime was discovered, he was unceremoniously released. Several years passed and I had opportunity to see him play on several occasions, though people always snickered when his name was mentioned.

Sweeney signed an autograph for me early on, which made me quite pleased since I always like to get top players to sign my scorebook or any of my prospect books. I was hoping to get Ruben Rivera to sign a couple of baseball cards that I still had from nearly a decade ago when I was a rabid sports card enthusiast. I brought five cards with me, three of which were of Rivera, and I was ready for him as he came out of the tunnel. "Hey, Ruben" yelled the Caucasian Grimace in his French-Canadian accent, a conglomeration of nasal English, frog-like French, and Native American staccato. Rivera approached wondering what exactly this odd man wanted. Rivera played for the Lynx a few years ago and the kindly fans of Ottawa always have something nice to say to former Lynx players. Rivera might have thought that perhaps this odd-looking man wanted to say hello or congratulate him on his recent play. I wished.

"Hey, Ruben, I've got a call for you," smiled the Caucasian Grimace, holding out his cell phone. "It's Derek Jeter. He wants his glove back."

I put my Ruben Rivera cards back in the plastic case.

"What did you say to me?" Rivera rhetorically asked, rage filling his face.

"Derek Jeter," Caucasian Grimace replied, pointing to the lower end of the cell phone. "He's on the phone and he wants his glove back."

Rivera then stalked over to the rail with a foreboding step and appeared as if he was ready to thrash the overweight menace. He swore numerous times, dropping f-bombs like Yogi Berra used malapropisms in interviews. Rivera even threatened to beat the hell (though it wasn't the word "hell") out of Caucasian Grimace in front of all of his friends. We (my friends Mark, Avi and I) tried to explain to Rivera that he should go right ahead and kick the crap out of him since he wasn't our friend anyway. I was clearly putting myself in harm's way with such a comment, since I was standing right next to the heckler. Eventually, after Rivera shoved Caucasian Grimace and it appeared the confrontation was about to get really ugly, a few players came out and restrained Rivera. Security came down and asked for some information, while my heckling "friend" said he did nothing, as he always does, because he is a weak man with no moral fiber. I can recall going to a game in Montreal where Mike Cameron made the heckler promise that he'd leave if he hit two home runs. By mid-game, Cameron had accomplished his goal and pointed to the Caucasian Grimace, who smiled but did not move.

After the fireworks ended between the heckler and Ruben Rivera, the game was played without issue. Hayden Penn, one of the top pitching prospects for the Orioles, made his Triple-A debut and pitched five shutout innings before he was pulled and Ottawa blew the game. Not that the fans in Ottawa noticed. Only a few hundred braved the cold weather (Charlotte manager Razor Shines, shivering in the dugout 10 minutes prior to the first pitch, proclaimed, "Man, you've got to be a fan to be here today"), and most of them were up in the restaurant watching the hockey game between the hometown Ottawa Senators and the defending Stanley Cup champion Tampa Bay Lightning. I'll admit, by the middle of the fourth I was in the restaurant myself, peering around poles to see the field while everyone else was eyeing the Senators game on the televisions above our heads. I was up there for warmth, but as one of the Lynx season-ticket holders so acutely said, "Only in Canada do people go to a baseball game and then pay more attention to hockey on a TV screen." He wasn't making fun of his countrymen, just stating a fact while sporting a Jason Spezza jersey, the first-line center of the Ottawa Senators.

Catching Lightning at a Ballpark

I could not help but think of the movie *The Great Outdoors*, with Dan Aykroyd and John Candy. While sitting in a bar, Aykroyd and Candy see an elderly man who has hair resembling a skunk. After some discussion, they discover he has been struck by lightning six times, but not really. The man stutters out that he was actually struck by lightning 66 times. In the head.

While sitting in the front row next to the bullpen on the first base side of Lynx Stadium, my friend Todd purchased ten 50-50 raffle tickets and exchanged pleasantries with the old lady selling the tickets. After completing their two-minute chat, she got up to leave and a foul ball was sent skyward on the first base side. It was over two sections and up about 25 rows, but apparently this was enough to send a jolt through her as she took a step back down the concrete steps, nearly falling into the row of seats behind us.

"Are you okay?" Todd asked.

"Oh, yes," she said as she steadied herself against the plastic back of an aisle seat. "I'm just a little jumpy. Last year I got hit seven times by foul balls."

"Seven times?" Todd replied incredulously. "You've got a better chance of getting hit by lightning four times."

If this were the case, according to my calculations, the skunk-locked man in the movie would have been struck by at least 115.5 foul balls during the 2005 season.

I found it absolutely amazing that this woman could be hit by seven foul balls over the course of one season. That is an absolutely amazing statistic. Over the last few seasons, I've been to several hundred professional games, another couple hundred amateur games, and I've sat in the stands at dozens of practices. Over the course of thousands of hours in harm's way, I've only been in the vicinity of half a dozen foul balls and on those occasions I was always an unmoving target. However, it does remind me of one of the greatest baseball stories ever. I believe it was Richie Ashburn, while playing for the Phillies in the 1950s, who sent a screaming line drive into the stands that hit a woman so severely that she needed to be carried off on a stretcher. During the same at bat, Ashburn sent another line drive to the same spot, hitting the woman again while she was being attended to by emergency staff. That story could be apocryphal, but nonetheless remains a personal favorite of mine.

A few notes of interest from this game before I describe one of the most hilarious sights ever witnessed on a diamond:

1) Ottawa continues to be an odd place. An Ottawa scorecard hawker was advertising his product by saying that some of them had Adam Stern autographs inside. Having signatures inside of the programs is certainly not out of the ordinary for most minor league parks, except for one detail: Stern played for the opposing team, Pawtucket. Stern is a Canadian, but come on. I can't wait to see what they do if Adam Loewen, another Canadian, but one who is actually in the Baltimore organization, comes to town.

2) After a pop up fell between two Ottawa infielders, a fan said it was like an Abbott and Costello routine. I'm fairly certain the famous "Who's on first" routine had nothing about infield pop flies. This is a nitpick, but "I've got it, you've got it," has nothing to do with the comedy shtick.

3) One of the fans in the adjacent section asked Pawtucket reliever Jermaine Van Buren if he was pinch-hitting. I'm sure (at least I hope I'm sure) that the fan meant to ask if he was going in to pitch, but it's Ottawa, so you never know.

4) The first base umpire asked Van Buren if he was a hockey fan. Only in Canada can an umpire ask a baseball player if he's a hockey fan. Clearly the umpire had other things on his mind.

Yes, clearly the umpire had other things on his mind. And not just the first base umpire, but the third base umpire and also the home plate umpire. Before going further, let me say that umpiring is one of the most unappreciated positions in sports. In fact, refereeing in general is so good at the professional level, the average fan can hardly comprehend it. How often do fans yell at Little League, high school or collegiate umpires? A great deal, because for the most part, they aren't good at the job. However, minor league umpires and major league umpires are outstanding. Unfortunately, the minor league umpires were on strike in the months of March, April and in to the month of May. Retired umpires and local upper level officials were called upon across the continent to take over until the strike was settled. There were a few flare ups around the minor leagues with some poor incidents, including Devil Rays prospect Delmon Young tossing his bat into the home plate umpire's chest in Pawtucket just a few days earlier. Apparently Pawtucket's club acts as a lightning rod for mismanaged officiating.

With one out in the top of the eighth inning, the score tied 4-4 and a runner at second base, the aforementioned Adam Stern was at the plate for the Paw Sox. The home plate umpire had really struggled all game with his strike zone, which was approximately the size of a tissue box. And it moved up and down, which is never good. Anyway, Ottawa's sidearm reliever Andy Mitchell threw a pitch that was right down the middle. Stern isn't a big man, but it looked like a strike at the belt. It was not called that way. Ball one. The next pitch was called a strike, but the following two pitches were called balls, making the count 3-1. After a few seconds, timeout was called by the home plate umpire who then had a meeting with his counterparts behind the mound. After some discussion, it was decided the count was 2-2, not 3-1. Clearly the home plate umpire fooled his partners so much that they thought the first pitch was a strike. The Pawtucket manager then captured the home plate umpire's attention and questioned him, causing further discussion between all three men in blue. It was then decided that the original tally, the count of 3-1, had been correct, forcing Dave Trombley, the Ottawa manager, to come out and argue. Todd actually took the time to grab my scorebook from me and was offering its use for the umpires from our front row position. Jermaine Van Buren, who had chatted with us for the last two innings, was quite amused by this generosity and said that the official scorer was right down here next to him in the bullpen and the umps should come over and check my coverage of the game. The three of us enjoyed a hearty laugh about the scorebook and the continuing perplexing issue on the field, but the real laughs were about to come.

On the next pitch, Adam Stern walked. The next batter, shortstop Dustin Pedroia, singled to score the go-ahead run. Trombley came storming out of the dugout shouting vulgarities and was immediately ejected by the third base umpire. He then threw his hat into the air and went *"Naked Gun"* on the umpires. He made a grand signal and threw the third base umpire out of the game, pointed to the second base umpire and threw him out of the game, and then wound up and emphatically tossed the home plate umpire out of the game with showmanship that would make NFL wide receivers Terrell Owens and Chad Johnson stand up and applaud. He returned to the dugout and set a new unofficial record for longest helmet toss, chucking a pair of Lynx helmets all the way to the pitcher's mound.

It just got out of control from that point.

In the bottom of the inning, catcher Eli Whiteside was struck out looking on a ball that nearly hit him, causing Alejandro Freire, who had reached first on a walk two batters earlier, to scream obscenities at the official and follow him back towards the dugout. He was calmed down and returned to his first base duties for the next inning, but clearly the umpires were no longer running the game, which became even more obvious when Dustin Pedroia was called out on a strike that was barely ankle high. Pedroia was equally incensed, swearing at both the home plate umpire and then the first base umpire when he tried to break things up. Pedroia continued his tirade in the bottom of the inning at his shortstop position when the first pitch short-hopped the catcher and Pedroia screamed, "strike!"

Unfortunately for Pedroia and the rest of the lightning rod Paw Sox, the minor league umpire's strike is still on and probably will be for a while. If this kind of shabby umpiring continues, it will only provide more ammunition for the real professionals who will be able to ask for virtually anything they desire.

Pathetic in Pink

Three weeks passed before I was able to travel to another remarkable baseball game, so my excuse is that my senses were dulled and my gullibility had returned to the heights of pre-adolescence. In the middle of the second inning, I thought Myrtle Beach Pelicans third baseman Van Pope was my new favorite minor league player. I have no definitive evidence, but I'm fairly certain I was a victim of the Blue Rock Flimflam.

In the gap between the great Trombley experience and the Blue Rock Flimflam, I endured the misfortune of a few waning weeks of work before my summer of leisure could commence. My job precludes me from attending as many games as I would like in the early months of the season. In a way it is a positive, for if it weren't for my work schedule in the first six weeks of the baseball campaign, I would be flat broke from travel costs. Seventeen days followed the Dave Trombley incident before I could attend another game. A fairly non-descript doubleheader in Ottawa in mid-May was the cure and I was excited to see a Hayden Penn-David Purcey pitching match up in game two of the twin bill. I also attempted to go to the Hall of Fame game between Pittsburgh and Cincinnati the previous Monday, but the contest was quickly rained out. The only remarkable item from that day, besides watching Adam Dunn deposit baseballs into Cooperstown suburbia during the pre-game home run derby, regarded a tractor that drove through the winding roads of central New York at 15 miles per hour with no area for passing. It was the antithesis of the Steven Spielberg movie *Duel*.

But now, late in May, my series of baseball sojourns were to truly begin. Staring at an early morning seven-hour drive to New Jersey, I'm pretty sure I sabotaged myself the previous night. The athletic department at Clarkson was losing one of its coaches to a different profession and there was an early-evening going-away party. Knowing full well to get up at 4 a.m. to drive a couple hundred miles I would need something to help me fall asleep earlier than usual, I downed a glass of red wine, hoping it would make me drowsy enough to get to sleep by 9 p.m. It didn't work and I ended up downing close to a bottle of wine on my own. When I made it home an hour later, I was about 50-50 of whether or not I could summon my body up in five hours to drive seven more to Lakewood, New Jersey, for a 1:05 start. A beeping noise shrieked from my cell phone at 3:30 a.m., indicating that I had received a text message. The artificial light blasted my half-closed eyes as I read a message from my friend Tim saying, "What's he doing in Detroit?" The groan that came from my throat after I read the fifth word made it evident that I had no intention of getting up in 30 minutes to drive. So I slept in, and the aforementioned Lakewood team would remain an unvisited location in my minor league travels.

However, when the newly set alarm blared a few hours later, I was ready to go to my second planned destination of the day, Wilmington, Delaware. Having visited Wilmington before, I was familiar with the parking and location of the ballpark, so I could make a leisurely drive through Pennsylvania. More importantly, I returned a text message to Tim that read, "Well, send him plane fare and a new pair of pants." If anyone knows this off the top of their head, we could be great friends.

I despise the roadways of Pennsylvania. It's the only thing that I dislike about the state; the landscape is picturesque, history abounds, and the state's alternate moniker of "Keystone" is shared with second base (the "keystone" sack for the uninformed), but driving through glorious PA is about as fun as banging your head against a redwood. In the span of 100 miles, I drove through a minimum of five road construction areas, none of which had anyone working. I know it was a Saturday, but we've got to come up with some shift work to get stuff done. I realize that money, labor laws, and other bureaucratic shiftiness get in the way, but can't we just put all of our petty differences aside and pave a freakin' road? Not to mention tolls were $6.25 for the 100 miles. For all of the traffic I encountered, I expect this road to be gilt-edged upon completion.

Once I arrived in Wilmington, it was reaffirmed to me why this franchise is considered one of the crown jewels of the Carolina League. Though it is not located in a high-end neighborhood and the traffic patterns for exiting are brutally idiotic, the park itself it astounding. On the outside, a statue of Hall of Famer and Negro League great Judy Johnson guards the entrance. On the inside, my favorite feature of any park was provided: an open concourse with a full view of the field. There is nothing less appealing to me in a ballpark than a concourse where you have to leave the view of the field. Any new stadium built with a sheltered concourse beneath the grandstand should be immediately demolished and the designer drawn and quartered. Or at the very least fired.

Wilmington employed several promotions for this particular Saturday in mid-May. A simplistic one was an orange baseball giveaway (Charlie O. Finley would be so proud), while another, as my friend Mike put it, looked like someone accidentally put a Red Sox hat in the wash with the white jerseys. Yes, the Wilmington Blue Rocks were wearing pink jerseys in recognition of breast cancer awareness. I'm all for awareness about cancer and the money raised for research, but I don't know if wearing hideous pink jerseys raises awareness. In fact, all it did was remind me of the time my older sister had a birthday party and she got sick and vomited up a bunch of pink cake at the bottom of our cellar stairs. The Strawberry Shortcake-themed party was designed to celebrate her eighth birthday, not traumatize me as a kindergartner. For the next two years, every time I went into the basement I hopped over the final concrete step and the three feet of open concrete before the rug was set down. Sure I was only a kid, but it obviously has had a significant effect on me. In addition to the pink jerseys, the Blue Rocks also placed pink bases on the field. As a traditionalist, I still have a moderately difficult time with major league baseball's wild card system and interleague play, so one can only imagine how I react to pink bases, no matter what the cause.

The final promotion was the appearance of something called Birdzirk. I must admit, I had never heard of this thing before, but it apparently is some kind of full-sized, wacky, traveling mascot that is a great draw for kids. After his first appearance, I must say that Birdzirk is entertaining for all.

In the middle of the second inning, Birdzirk was brought out on a four-wheeler and dropped off on the third base side where it began its stunts. Birdzirk enthusiastically hopped off the four-wheeler, danced around on the infield cut out, and then kicked Myrtle Beach third baseman Van Pope squarely in the seat of the pants while his back was turned. Pope reacted with some surprise, as I'm sure that getting kicked in the ass while fielding groundballs is not part of his regular routine during infield warm ups. Birdzirk then continued his dance out in front of Pope, where the youngster returned a kick to the keester of the mascot. With a quick turn around, Birdzirk and Pope were face to face and the mascot challenged Pope by dancing in front of him. Pope initially held off, but then dropped his glove and started competing with the mascot. I was gleeful. This, after all, was what minor league baseball was all about; learning the game, but being young and playful at the same time. The two went at it for about 30 seconds, but then the Myrtle Beach pitcher emerged from the dugout and appeared ready to go, so Birdzirk fled the scene on his four-wheeler, but with a souvenir: Van Pope's glove. Pope looked to retrieve his mitt by chasing the mascot into the outfield, but the Birdzirk flung it over the wall. One of the Pelicans' bench players came out with a pair of gloves and Pope fit one neatly on his non-throwing hand and was ready for the game to resume.

If I haven't mentioned it already, I adore foreshadowing. I just knew as Van Pope looked at his new glove and pounded the pocket with his fist, something involving the young third baseman was bound to occur this inning. More importantly, the delay seemed to agitate Pelicans pitcher Kelvin Vila. He pitched well enough to get out of the inning without a run, but a dropped fly ball was followed by two consecutive hits, including a groundball down the third base line that skimmed off Pope's glove and into shallow left field. Perhaps with Pope's regular glove he would have reached the grounder. Wilmington scored three times in the second and never looked back in a 6-1 win with the Blue Rocks pitching staff holding Myrtle Beach to just one hit through the first six innings.

Right around that point, Birdzirk re-emerged and began berating the home plate umpire with his dancing antics. The umpire, a younger guy, initially dismissed the mascot, but then complied with the giant bird and the two began yet another dance contest on the grass behind home plate. It was at this point that I believe I was duped by Van Pope. The umpire and Birdzirk seemingly knew all of the same moves, which I probably could have overlooked. When the umpire did a back flip, I was appalled. Thirty seconds later when an older, heavier umpire was on the first base line watching the final warm up pitches before the start of the inning, my heart sank just a bit. If the mascot has gimmicks, that's one thing, but this contrived display bothered me a great deal. Say it ain't so, Van, say it ain't so! At least, as he was a member of the visiting team, he wasn't forced to wear a pink jersey.

Pink bases, pink uniforms. Back when I was ultra competitive, I'd say don't ditch the pink jerseys until you lose. Now that I'm older and the occasional loss doesn't send me into a sputtering tirade of frustration, I say put them on Ebay and hope that someone wants to adorn their recreation room with a pink motif. Twenty years ago it would have gone well with the spatter on my basement floor.

Biggest Bean I've Ever Seen

When I was younger I didn't travel a lot, something I certainly lament now with gas at its current inflated cost. In my early 20s, I could have easily watched numerous minor leaguers who are all-stars now and likely will have plaques affixed in Cooperstown twenty years from now.

My visit to RFK Stadium the day after Wilmington was the first time I ever went to Washington, DC. It's probably not the key item on the tour for many visiting the most powerful city in the world, and it shouldn't be. With more time, I would have liked to have visited the Smithsonian and some national monuments. Instead I sat in a football stadium to watch two baseball games.

The first was the so-called "Battle of the Beltway," an alliterative title to a dull series. The Washington Nationals hosting the Baltimore Orioles at RFK needed some kind of extra promotion as the two teams were floundering well out of the playoff race, even with only 40 games expired from the season. In all honesty, the game lacked interesting points to notate. Again, my friend Mike attended with me, along with his wife, Andrea, and my friend Katie. Katie's utter lack of knowledge of the game was amusing, but I've always been patient with neophytic baseball fans in explaining the nuances of the sport. She was confused as to why players were sitting on the other side of the fence (the bullpen) and she shook her head in disbelief at what she perceived to be my neurosis for keeping score pitch-by-pitch. After a half inning I told her it was okay to talk to me during the game, I could keep track of pitch counts and keep score while holding a conversation as I've practiced this art in well over 500 games. She seemed relieved.

With the completion of the Orioles-Nationals contest, which Washington won 3-1, a minor league game began between the Nationals' single-A affiliate, Potomac, and the Salem Avalanche. Again, a very unremarkable game. It was, at the very least, an absolute opposite of the major league game, which saw four runs scored over nine innings, as both Potomac and Salem scored four runs in the third inning alone. Save for what I thought was an outstanding pitching match up, this game lacked the fervor of the first few games that I witnessed in Ottawa. Clint Everts, a former first-round pick and Tommy John surgery alum, started for the Nationals while Troy Patton started for the Avalanche. But it wasn't Patton. According to my roster and the electronic scoreboard, Patton was pitching for Salem. Of course, the pitcher was African-American. My previous experience, though limited, had proven to me that Patton was, in fact, white. Other than some laughable *Soul Man* gaff, two players had exchanged numbers. At some point in the third inning, I learned the pitcher was Ronnie Martinez. It really didn't matter since the quality-pitching match up for which I yearned had already dissolved into a slugfest. I hoped for a more interesting game in my return to New York on Monday.

While the games at RFK lacked any particular punch, the best part of the entire trip came when we returned to Mike's apartment. Late in the nationally-televised interleague game between the New York Mets and New York Yankees, youngster Colter Bean entered the game for the Yankees. Bean is a big man, probably around 6'6" and weighing well over 250 pounds. ESPN play-by-play announcer Jon Miller, as he sometimes does with unknown players, became fascinated with Bean's name. He repeated it close to a dozen times in the half inning, putting emphasis on the hard sounds of the name. I almost felt bad for his broadcasting partner, Hall of Fame second baseman Joe Morgan. I pictured the two of them having dinner together later and I could only imagine the exchange:

Morgan: Wow, that looks like some pretty good soup, Jon. What kind is it?

Miller: *Colter Bean.*

Morgan: That's interesting, I've never heard of that kind of soup before. Three-bean soup, black bean soup, sure, but never colter bean. Oh, Jon, it looks like you spilled some on your shirt. That's too bad, it looks like a nice shirt. Where did you get it?

Miller: *Colter Bean.*

Morgan: Colter Bean? I get catalogues from them all the time. They are out of Maine, right? Did they change names? I thought it was L.L. Bean. I usually look through those catalogues when I'm drinking coffee at home. By the way, what kind of coffee was that we had this morning at the hotel? That was delicious.

Miller: *Colter Bean.*

Morgan: Is that Columbian?

Lastings Milledge and the Financial Scams of Curt Schilling

Entering the 2006 season, over a three-year span of attending more than 170 games, I've acquired more than 700 autographs from over 400 different players. Already, close to 200 of those players have reached the major leagues and some have become stars, including Miguel Cabrera, David Wright, Joe Mauer, Chase Utley, Travis Hafner, Grady Sizemore, and Frank Thomas (rehab assignment in 2005). Others will certainly become stars, like Jeff Francoeur, BJ Upton, Jose Reyes, Justin Verlander, Ryan Howard, Scott Kazmir, and Francisco Liriano. However, in 2006, I've already found myself not wanting to ask players for their signatures. Call it maturity or call it embarrassment, it's something that doesn't hold the same kind of draw that it once did. Unless of course I'm in the presence of a stud like Lastings Milledge. Then all bets are off.

Milledge, a first-round pick of the Mets in the 2003 draft was a consensus first-round talent. He somehow slipped to the 12th overall pick that year despite tools that rivaled those of number one overall choice Delmon Young. Some questioned the personal makeup of Milledge since there were allegations of sexual misconduct with a younger girl while he was in high school. Upon first reading, it's obvious how that would rub some teams the wrong way. Of course, we are a headline society and only see the larger statement rather than the story that goes along with it. Sure, Milledge was with a younger girl, but it was his girlfriend, who just happened to be about two years younger than him. If we were to arrest every kid who has engaged in underage sex, no one would ever be able to leave the country and the prisons would be loaded with a very significant portion of today's youth. The famous line would ring true: the meek (or the geek) would inherit the earth.

Furthermore, what is even more startling is that the Mets were torn between Milledge and prep pitcher Jeff Allison. Though he was thought to be a can't-miss high school pitching prospect, or at least as can't-miss as a high school pitcher can be, Allison has struggled with drug addiction, first with pain-killers and then with harder narcotics. I've met Jeff Allison and he seems like a nice enough kid. I hope he gets his life straightened around and then takes care of baseball matters, should he so choose. It just proves that teams can employ all of the psychological tests that they want, but baseball players aren't unalterable machines and the human mind and spirit is a very unpredictable thing.

I saw Milledge play for the first time in the 2005 Futures Game at Comerica Park in Detroit. Not much to comment about with that one at bat he had in the seven-inning game, but I watched him play in Binghamton two times in late-July, once again in August up in Maine, and then again at Binghamton in late-August. His bat speed is impressive, his ability to track a ball in centerfield is smooth, and he runs like a deer. He is the only player I've ever seen try a straight steal of home, against a right-handed pitcher no less, though he was caught. He is one of the five most exciting players I've seen in minor league baseball over the last four years, and I was worried he would be in the majors or traded to another team before I was able to see him play in person in 2006.

The schedule and the Mets cooperated, keeping Milledge in the minors in late-May in Syracuse, NY. Alliance Bank Stadium, the newly re-named ballpark of the Syracuse Sky Chiefs, is a funny place. It's just outside the city and very easy to get to, located less than a mile from the Carousel Mall, and the park is quite nice on the outside. Inside it has that hideous turf that was en vogue in the 1980s and employs a lot of those really annoying metal bars to separate aisles and seats. Though the inside cosmetics do not give Alliance Bank Stadium any edge over other parks, it can be an okay place to watch a game, were it not for the fans. With plenty of games under my belt at P&C Stadium (the name of Alliance Bank for all but the last two seasons) over the years, I have ample experience from which to draw upon. In numerous conversations, I've found the fans to be neither knowledgeable nor intelligent, and not even pleasant. A friend of mine named Scott went to watch Pawtucket play at Syracuse during the 2005 season when Curt Schilling was on his rehabilitation assignment. He told me a most amusing story that he had with a supposed former grounds crew worker. The grounds crew worker disliked Sky Chiefs owner Tex Simone and said numerous disparaging remarks about him. A recounted conversation regarding Curt Schilling's rehab stint:

Groundskeeper: "Schilling won't pitch tonight."

Scott: "He's warming up right now in the bullpen to pitch an inning."

Groundskeeper: "No. It's all a big scam between Simone and Schilling. All of these people come and they'll split the gate. That way everybody has to come back tomorrow and the Sky Chiefs get twice the ticket sales. He'll pitch tomorrow."

A few minutes later, Schilling popped out of the bullpen and threw a seven-pitch inning for his rehab assignment. So much for the $20,000 financial windfall for Curt Schilling. I suppose he'll just have to take solace in his eight-figure yearly contract. Scott went on to let me know that the former grounds crew worker was a "close" friend of John Smoltz and that the Braves' former Cy Young Award winner pulled in "about" $150,000 a year. Perhaps he was confused. According to my calculations, Smoltz earned that monetary amount per save in 2004.

The fans of Syracuse also tend to scream incoherent comments at players with unnecessary vulgarity and regularity. You can't fault hecklers for trying to get under the skin of the opposition, but it would be so much better if the Syracuse people were clever instead of just saying "you suck." And from my experience, the kids in attendance are the type of fans who think it is a birthright to receive a baseball from the players once they cross through the turnstiles, shouting at players when a ball isn't tossed in their direction.

Syracuse has a rabid group of autograph hunters, and though I was one of the first people into the stadium when it opened at 6:05, there were already a handful of guys down by the first base dugout. Knowing the routine in this stadium, I casually walked down to the spot. My pace quickened when I saw that Milledge was already down there signing autographs and there were only a couple of people in his visibility. Fortunately, Milledge obliged by signing both a Mets mini-helmet and a Binghamton Mets hat that was given out as a promotion in 2005. From my previous history with Milledge, he would sign only one autograph per person, so one of my friends took care of the mini-helmet while I took the Binghamton hat. Terrible autograph, but when you have a name as long as Lastings Milledge, you shorten the signature. Forty-five minutes later when warm ups were nearly complete, I decided to get greedy in hopes that Milledge would stop over again and I was rewarded when he sidled up to the first row of seats and began grabbing more items from the throng of autograph seekers that had now grown to over 30. My friend Scott came again and he had an 8x10 autographed for me while Milledge signed my *Baseball America* Prospect Handbook. A solid night of autographs from one of the elite prospects in the game.

Though the game required extra innings with the Tides winning 3-2 in 11 frames, the Sky Chiefs' fans were remarkably tame. It wasn't until late in the game when the catcalls came for Milledge and numerous other Norfolk players, many from the same fans that he had graciously signed for just a few hours earlier. When in Syracuse, I would expect little else.

I've Seen Fire
and I've Seen Rain

A Bloody Mary maybe, but beer at 10 a.m. on a Thursday? I felt like calling Alcoholics Anonymous. The worst part of watching someone drink several beers before noon in the middle of the week was that it was in full view of approximately 5,000 screaming elementary students. An early June game in Binghamton, NY, was the third installment of "Education Day" at the ballpark, allowing several thousand youngsters a day off from school. I'm not really sure what the education part of this day was. I know that when I went on road trips as a child, it was usually to a museum, concert, play, or a fun park that was a throwback to the 18th century.

Though I do appreciate the chance to see two games in one day, and a morning game always gives me enough time to drive to another park in the vicinity to set up my own kind of doubleheader, the education day promotion is usually the cause for the opportunity, forcing me into a situation that could transform itself into *Lord of the Flies* at any moment, flush with violence and anarchy. I've been to a dozen of these education days and only twice have I seen anything remotely close to learning at the ballpark. Once at Double-A Norwich of the Eastern League, an early game had about 2,000 students at the park for a drug awareness promotion. A drug-sniffing and well-trained German Shepherd gave the kids a thrill with all of the tricks he could do, but not before the officers gave a speech to those in attendance about the dangers of drugs. Another game in Ottawa had several science experiments in the concourse, though the booths were not as well attended as the concession stands. This masquerade of education scares me and makes me wonder if students in Japan are eating nachos and ice cream at 11:00 a.m. while sitting at a Sumo wrestling event. Somehow, I doubt it.

Now for the guy drinking beer at 10 a.m. on a Thursday. It's not like this was Patriots' Day in Boston when the Red Sox host a game at 11 a.m. in Fenway Park while the Boston Marathon is simultaneously run; for the most part that is a regional holiday with numerous people given the day off. Some random day in the middle of the week is not the cause for celebration and beer. Also, if it is the "Education at the Ballpark" promotion, perhaps someone should shut down the beer taps for the day while the 5,000 kids are running around. I half expected one of the teachers to be doing a keg stand.

While I may be venting over these two things at Binghamton, they do happily bring back to memory my favorite moment ever at a ballpark. Between games of a rainy doubleheader in New Haven, Connecticut, two years before the team moved to New Hampshire, the local Ravens were taking on the same Mets of Binghamton. My friend Tim and I were stalking Jose Reyes of the Mets as he and the rest of the team were doing a mini-tour of New England in August. In the matter of just a few minutes, I witnessed some of the most hilarious things I could ever see at a ballpark. Tim wanted a drink and I longed for an Italian Ice as we walked through the concourse at old Yale Field. The park was antiquated, and everyone had to walk under the stands like some kind of cheap prehistoric high school field. And I mean everyone. The visitor's clubhouse was right at the main entrance of the park and the players had to walk through the stands to get to the field. Speedster Esix Snead, since made famous in 2005 when he hurled his batting helmet and subsequently attacked David Bush from behind during an International League game, apparently wasn't happy with the spread in the clubhouse. He came out, in full uniform, and stood in line at one of the concession stands to get a soda. A boy, around seven or eight years old, came up to him with a baseball and asked him for an autograph. Snead calmly put his soda down, signed the ball for the boy, picked up his soda and slurped on it for a minute or so, surveying the concourse while a few hundred people milled down the hallway for food. He sidled back to the clubhouse entrance and disappeared behind the door. He missed the real show.

Within 30 seconds, out of the corner of my eye, I saw a six-foot Raven, in full costume, lugging a keg of beer into the concession stand. Sure, it's minor league baseball and everyone has to lend a hand. Sure, a mascot can't disappoint the kids and cut through the wall separating fantasy and reality by taking off part of the costume for manual labor. But a six-foot Raven struggling to carry a keg of beer from the side room, especially after having just slipped on a slick dugout roof, thanks to a rainy night, and nearly tumbling onto the field of play, that is just too much to handle. I will forever embrace this as the watershed moment when I realized that the overall spectacle of minor league baseball far outweighed anything that the majors could possibly provide. I've seen cycles, near no-hitters, momentous home runs and some of the greatest players to ever put on uniforms in the major leagues, but it bears repeating: nothing will ever top a six-foot Raven hauling brew for a couple of drunk middle-aged men demanding more Coors Lite.

All this said, in 200 games of professional baseball over the last three-plus seasons, I don't think I've had one alcoholic drink. Sixty helpings of nachos, 50 hot dogs, 25 chicken finger platters, 120 sodas, 30 bags of popcorn, a meatball sub and one very bland philly chicken cheesesteak, but no booze. It's sacrilegious to some, but normal for me. I have a scorebook to deal with, players to scout, and people to talk to. Add that to the fact that I have to drive several hours to and from games, and it is difficult to imbibe.

After the B-Mets game, I drove to Connecticut for a New Britain Rockcats game which was to be followed by the San Francisco Giants taking on the New York Mets at Shea Stadium on Friday. The weather was supposed to cooperate for the remainder of my trip.

However, after a few hours driving through southern New York and across I-84 into Connecticut, a cloud of evil hung in the sky, making it appear to be night though it was not yet 5 p.m. Twenty miles from New Britain, it was not raining, but lightning lit the blackened sky in one of the most awesome performances by Mother Nature that I've ever seen. Bolts shrieked across the sky to my left, to my right and directly in front of me. The squiggles of electricity burst once every few seconds. I held out hope, but I knew I was rained out for the second game of my two-city doubleheader. No matter, I would just catch the Rockcats on Saturday or Sunday when the weather cleared. Little did I know that somewhere in southern Connecticut weathermen were bent over in hearty laughter, mocking my dreams of dry baseball.

Admittedly, the weather looked dreary for Queens on Friday, but it couldn't rain. It was Pedro Martinez t-shirt giveaway day and, more importantly, this was my only chance to see Barry Bonds in 2006. That may not seem like much, but I haven't seen Barry Bonds play in person since 2001 and, damn it, I'm going to see him play. Bonds is my favorite player and has been since the Pirates actually won games back in the late-80s and early-90s.

Without getting on a soap box like every other writer in America, I'm going to briefly discuss Bonds and my thoughts on the steroid controversy: I don't care. I don't care if he knowingly or unknowingly took steroids. He was a Hall of Famer before anyone ever accused him of taking steroids. I don't care if any major league players took steroids in the 1990s and early 21st century. At the time, there were no rules against steroids or amphetamines, so how can anyone possibly get on a moral high horse and question competitive athletes? For decades, players have cheated in a variety of ways. Players gulped down greenies and red juice in the 1950s, 60s and 70s like vitamins and orange juice to get extra pep. Are we to question Willie Mays's statistics because of his potential use of amphetamines? Players have been juicing their arms with cortisone shots for decades. Heck, Sandy Koufax spent the last two years of his career being shot up with "performance enhancing" painkillers. It is well-documented that Koufax couldn't lift his arm in between starts because of the intense pain and swelling. How is cortisone different than a steroid, really? This is simply a technological jump, so it doesn't matter to me.

The steroid controversy is reminiscent of the 17th-century Salem witch trials and ripe with 1950s McCarthyism, full with its own senate hearings and trials. The whole thing is a joke. The only reason anybody happens to care about steroids in baseball is because of the historical aspect of the sport and the perceived increase of strength, allowing for baseballs to be hit farther. The collective mind's eye of baseball fans always remembers players at their best, through stories that were written by hero-worship journalism and storytelling. It's why no power hitter will ever be greater than Babe Ruth, why no hitter will ever be better than Ted Williams, or why no athlete will ever be greater than Willie Mays. Yet, somehow, the players and athletes are far superior to the greats of yesteryear in *every* other sport. For anyone who thinks performance-enhancers are absent in the other professional sports, they are not only naïve, but they are stupid, and the public outcry in the other major sports is miniscule.

I enjoy watching baseball games. If hitters hit the juice really hard in the late-1990s to further my enjoyment, fine. I'm over it, and I wish everyone else would get over it, too. The rules are now in place to prevent any further occurrences of rampant cheating, so sportswriters and radio talking heads can now calm down. Besides, it's not like hitters were the only players supposedly taking more than Flintstones vitamins.

All that being said, I really wanted to see Barry Bonds' giant melon wearing a helmet and swinging from the left side of the batter's box.

I missed seeing Bonds play for three straight years. In 2003, I would have seen Bonds in Montreal, but his father passed away and he went on the bereavement list during the Giants' only trip north of the border. In 2004, I bought tickets to Shea Stadium in hopes of seeing Bonds. He had the sniffles, so he was out of the lineup that night, but the night was redeemed because USA softball star Jennie

Finch was there and that somehow made it all right.* In 2005, again I purchased tickets for Shea in hopes of seeing Bonds in early June. His numerous knee injuries kept that from being possible. I couldn't miss him again.

But I did.

On the early drive from Connecticut towards New York City, it began to mist a little. Within 20 minutes it was raining. Twenty minutes later it was a downpour. Thirty minutes more it was a deluge. By the time cars were crossing the Whitestone Bridge, 18-inch deep puddles were forming on the side of the road causing an entire lane of traffic to veer into the center lanes. And this was only the beginning.

The rain slowed to a constant drizzle as we exited towards Shea Stadium. Driving through the Flushing area, small lakes formed on the sides of the road. My friend Tim's Honda Civic barreled through the huge puddles without problems. The worst appeared to be over until we neared the Shea Stadium parking lot past Flushing Meadows-Corona Park. Fifty-foot long puddles that were at least two feet deep held enough water to remind me of flooding footage I've seen on the Weather Channel during hurricane season. Tim expertly drove through the first puddle as water splashed on both sides of the car. Other cars raced through the puddles in hopes of not getting stuck while we eased our way on to dry road. Tim, another friend, Tommy, and myself breathed a collective sigh of relief, until we turned the corner where a longer, seemingly deeper puddle lie in wait. We held the air in our lungs until we made it through the second puddle. Again, we were not done. A seventy-five foot puddle in which ducks could set up shop for several days had collected beneath an overpass, but we could not be deterred. As Tim plunged the Honda Civic into thigh-deep water for a third time, all I could think of was what kind of water-born diseases I would get when I had to crawl out

---

* *Jennie Finch talked with Bonds for at least 15 minutes during batting practice and she was not dwarfed by Bonds at all. I wonder if she is on the juice.*

Tim's side windows to push his car out of the puddle. Typhoid? Diphtheria? Dysentery? Or would I only inhale the garbage surrounding the parking lot or lingering near drains. Used condoms? Plastic baggies? Chewing gum? The endless possibilities in a city of 10 million people were intriguing, but I really just wanted Tim to make it through the puddle. The water crested over the top of the hood of the car as smoke started coming from the engine. Oh shit, was pretty much all I could think. Somehow, we made it through this outlet of Little Neck Bay and I thought it would be smooth sailing from then on. If only we'd had a boat. The next puddle looked as if you could go snorkeling and spot odd water life that only Steve Zissou could dream up.

"Tim, no," I pleaded. It wasn't even my car and I didn't think it could take any more. "Turn right here."

Tim obliged, and we drove to a distant parking lot where there was only a foot-deep puddle waiting for us. Mere child's play! The rain had slowed to a sprinkle and my hopes of seeing Bonds increased. He probably wouldn't start, but he might get to pinch-hit late in the game.

The three of us stood under the cover of Shea Stadium for the next 45 minutes, dreaming of when we could enter the ballpark, but it simply wasn't meant to be. At about 5:30 p.m., the game was called and rescheduled as a doubleheader on Saturday. In a baseball world where every penny counts and team's look to gain as much revenue as possible, the Mets were going to play an old-fashioned doubleheader where a ticket holder actually got to stay for both games, not a day-night doubleheader (two games, two sets of tickets) that has been in vogue for the past 15 years. The team was offering exchanges or refunds for the Friday ticket holders, all the while still accepting money from those who wished to park their cars in the adjoining lots. With a $100 million payroll and numerous other cash cow revenues, you would think the team could afford some walkie-talkies to inform the parking attendants that they were, in effect, stealing money from the fans. I found the free doubleheader for Saturday ticket holders and the parking situation to be an interesting contradiction in moneymaking methodology.

The drive back to Connecticut was uneventful, though it was amusing to watch my friend Tommy see if he could hold back his desire to use a restroom (apparently the dripping water had played games with his brain and urinary tract), as the rain slowed to a stop for an hour or two. So I wasn't going to see Bonds during the weekend. No problem. It wouldn't be a total loss as I could always just go see the Rockcats on Saturday.

Somewhere in Connecticut the weathermen started wiping away tears of laughter. Their sides were already so sore that abdominal workouts would be unnecessary for days.

Thunderstorms and rain continued to bury the already flooded state of Connecticut all day on Saturday. A doubleheader was scheduled at New Britain after two consecutive rainouts. The number increased to three and I had enough. I set a land speed record for fastest drive through the Adirondack Mountains that night. I just wanted to get home. With all the food and gas purchased I, in essence, dropped $150 on a minor league baseball game in Binghamton, NY.

Those chortling Connecticut weathermen had best hope they never run into me on the street.

The Longest Day

It wasn't so much being held hostage as it was delving into the underbelly of a cult that a relative recently joined. You could leave any time you wanted, but you could never come back inside. After a while it became a matter of principle. Arriving at Fenway Park in a mild drizzling rain at 11:45 a.m. for a 1:20 p.m. start is, under normal (i.e. sunny) circumstances, late in my eyes. The fact that the game was delayed for nearly five hours until Jon Lester threw his first major league pitch at 6:12 p.m. proved that I was grossly early. Of course there are worse places to be stuck than Fenway Park, like the Department of Motor Vehicles or a dentist's chair. However, bridgework at the dentist's office is sometimes cheaper than a run to the concession stand at Fenway Park.

There are only three stadiums remaining in major league baseball that are universally adorned with praise from players, old-time fans, kids, and media members: Yankee Stadium, Wrigley Field and Fenway Park. It helps that each is more than 80 years old, supplying nostalgia for the baby boomers and, of course, providing down-time fodder for unimaginative broadcasters who are dumbing down the banter with their booth partners so much that the 10-year-olds listening have heard the stories 20 times. Fenway Park gets that treatment, but it is deserved. The park itself lacks a lot of things that fans appreciate in the modern world. Getting to your seat can be a hassle because the walkways between sections are miniscule and only offer enough room for two or maybe three people to walk abreast. If one arrives at the park close to game time, maneuvering in the underlying concourse is hardly a treat, despite the fact that nearly everyone knows where he or she is going. Also, the seats themselves are wooden and uncomfortable, not only because of their wood framing, but because the rows themselves are placed inches apart. I could tolerate wooden seats, but my knees curse me at the end of a game at Fenway, creaking and cracking with the first 100 steps I take, having been pounded by the seat in front of me. If only I drank beer and made numerous runs to the concession stands, I could probably work the kinks out.

Originally, I had no intention of going to the game on June 10th, especially since I already owned tickets for June 11th. A couple of phone conversations convinced me otherwise. A friend (Steve) of a friend (Ryan) had tickets and was looking for a compatriot for the afternoon game. The spots were only standing room, but at least I wouldn't be sitting for three hours.

Instead, I'd be standing for eight.

I arrived in Brighton, my residence for a year, which is located just a short 57-bus ride from Fenway. It was early, about 10:45 a.m., and the nearly six-hour drive had left me fatigued. I walked upstairs to Steve's place and sat down to watch Sportscenter in between weather updates. While the rain was sprinkling off and on, it appeared as if the game should go on without too much issue. It takes a lot to call off a major league game, due to the price of tickets. Waiting for the latest climatic update, Steve and I spent some time bantering about recent Red Sox draft picks. He had read about them, but never saw any of them play, so I was able to fill in the gaps regarding each player's talent as opposed to the bloggers he was reading who likely perused a scouting report, looked up the stats and concluded that Michael Bowden was the next Roger Clemens. The internet is a wonderful thing, but it has also doubled as the ultimate corruptor of the general public's mind.

Following 30 minutes of Red Sox chatter, Steve and I departed the shelter of his apartment and hopped on the bus to the stadium. We got off at Kenmore Square and walked the couple hundred yards to Fenway where a smattering of fans wandered around the park.

Normally this group would be considerably more robust, but I didn't give it much thought. Steve got a beer, a refrain that will be repeated a few times.

The field was draped when we got inside, the tarp clinging to the grass and infield cut outs like a wet t-shirt to a co-ed during spring break, providing an outline that shows a glimpse of its beauty underneath. Little to no activity was occurring at field level and that certainly concerned me, especially when Steve, on his second beer, told me that the Red Sox would not take off the tarp until the rain totally stopped.

"What?" I said.

"Yeah, it's there policy not to remove the tarp until it's stopped," Steve explained. "Before the game it can't be raining at all and then they will start."

I was slightly dismayed by this discovery as water continued to mist down on to the field, wondering if I would make my nighttime appointment in Allston, another suburb of Boston. Steve turned as he received a call on his cell phone. His friend Olivia was at the other end of his conversation and just happened to be attending the pre-game as well, so we went to meet her behind home plate for a drink, since our spots on the standing room bar seemed safe for the time being.

For the next 90 minutes we remained behind home plate with Steve, Olivia, and a guy whose name escaped me about three seconds after he said it making runs to and from the beer stand while I watched helplessly at the rain continually falling from the sky. I looked on anxiously as other games across the eastern seaboard began. Somehow, it was sunny in New York City as the Yankees took on the Athletics. If the Red Sox had not won the World Series in 2004, I would have thought that ironic, but that one magnificent incident has really changed Boston and New England baseball fans quite profoundly.

Somewhere around 2:30, the group decided to leave the ballpark's concourse and go into the accompanying bar, Who's On First. Steve ordered beers along with a rum and coke and his speech began to slur. Truly, who was on first, what was on second, and I don't know was on third because Steve was getting loaded.

By 3:15, with the game in its first two hours of delay, I was back outside in the streets dodging the few, minimal sprinkles that fell from the gray sky. I ran through the concourse to see if any action was being taken on the field as far as the removal of the tarp. Not a soul was to be seen on the playing surface and I was beginning to become anxious. As a result, I decided to calm myself by filling out a handful of all-star game ballots. Or maybe two hundred.

Sitting directly by the all-star ballot stand, I monotonously took one ballot, poked the appropriate holes, folded it back up and placed it in the receptacle. For an hour. A few players received my vote each and every time while others were selected sparingly. I even created themes for certain ballots. On one, I picked every single Boston Red Sox player, and in the National League selected players who recently played for the Sox. Anything to keep myself amused. I'm not even a huge Red Sox fan, but I felt that I should support the locals.

While supporting one group of locals, my amusement with another, Steve, was wearing thin. When one person is sloshed and the other is stone sober, the situation resembles the odd couple. He wanted to leave since it was closing in on 5:00 p.m. and he spent all $80 with which he came to the park, along with the $30 I had delivered for the ticket. He checked with several attendants on the possibility of re-entering the park when the game started, but the scanning system with which tickets are taken did not allow for this in any situation. It truly was quite the racket. The Red Sox allowed fans to come inside the gates to drink beer and eat gastrocolic nightmares, but had yet to provide any sort of on-field entertainment for six hours. In the ballclub's defense, this game was supposed to be the first in a day-night doubleheader because a game in May was rained out and the team didn't want to call off this game again, forcing this ravenous fan base to return to the park a third time for further wallet gouging. For several hours, I overheard passersby praying for the Sox to call the game so they could just go home, but no one wanted to just leave after paying $50 for a ticket and countless other dollars at the concession and souvenir stands. I knew I sure as hell wasn't going anywhere.

I was rewarded for my patience. Around 5:30 or so, the grounds crew began its work on removing the wet t-shirt off the infield, and the crowd began to cheer at the striptease. I really felt for Jon Lester, the top pitching prospect in the Red Sox farm system. Here it was his major league debut and he had to sit in the clubhouse for six hours waiting for the rain to cease. The nervousness that the average major leaguer has in his debut is considerable, but at least they get to go out and take batting practice to loosen up or play a little long toss. Lester was stuck listening to music or playing cards with a bunch of guys he didn't know all that well, save for some time spent with the team in spring training.

He didn't show any ill effects when he faced his first batter at 6:12 pm, only 4 hours and 52 minutes later than expected. He struck out Texas leadoff hitter Gary Matthews, Jr. on four pitches and received a standing ovation from the "sellout" crowd. He promptly gave up a double off the left field wall to Michael Young. The hitting machine shortstop officially welcomed him to the show. It brought a smile to my face, seeing this kid who was barely of legal drinking age enjoy both success and failure within two minutes. A strikeout and a piss-rod to the fence in the course of two minutes. It's a great game.

Steve wasn't there to see it. Nearly broke, drunk, and bordering on incoherent if not inconsolable, Steve stumbled out through the gates to return home at about quarter after five, head on a swivel, looking for a bus or a cab which he would be unable to pay for.

Just another satisfied customer and proud member of Red Sox Nation.

Visiting the King

Baseball aficionados are aware of the exploits of Mike Kelly, but unfortunately his feats have been long forgotten by the average fan. The first true superstar of baseball, there were players with similar or perhaps even superior skill, but his flair for the game was unmatched. His style of play fit the fast-paced, hard-drinking early days of the sport in the 19th century and his personality allowed fans and writers to adorn him with the title "King."

Kelly was one of the great innovators in baseball and his quick wits allowed him to circumvent many of the rules of the day. With only one umpire overseeing the game, he sometimes would skip bases and run across the infield without touching each one while the arbiter was in the outfield with his back turned. Another famous tale includes Kelly substituting himself for the catcher in the middle of a pop fly so that he could record an out, again dodging the parameter of the rules. In addition to those somewhat underhanded methods of play, he also pioneered the hit-and-run, the concept of catchers backing up first base on balls in the infield and the hook slide. Like other great players after him, the game was changed because of his play, and his originality is legendary.

Unfortunately, Kelly, who also happened to be the first player ever sold for a five-figure sum, lived his life in the same manner in which he played the game: at an obscenely fast pace. His prodigious drinking ability was just one of his destructive qualities that likely sent him to an early grave. Kelly was a year beyond his major league baseball playing days when, just two months shy of his 37th birthday, he fell ill and passed away from pneumonia in late 1894. After three seasons as skipper, he certainly could have enjoyed an impressive managerial run, much in the same way John McGraw did just a decade later, had he lived to see the 20th century.

Destructive qualities aside, this man has always fascinated me despite our lives being set a century apart. His education was feeble, but he embodied the American Dream before the white-picket-fence model existed. The son of immigrants who came to the United States in the middle of the 19th century to work in textile mills, he, too, appeared likely to endure a hard life, selling newspapers and working mills in his early years before discovering a talent for hitting a ball with a bat in a superior manner to all of the other boys his age. His odd talent was likely beyond the comprehension of his parents or anyone else in his native Ireland, for baseball was truly nothing more than a child's game and life in the 19th century was that of intense back-breaking labor, not prolonged leisure. It is that which embodies the American Dream: gaining renowned success in the unknown. How many hundreds of thousands of immigrants came to the United States hoping for a better life, never knowing what personal triumphs or horrors they would encounter. In the case of Mike Kelly, he would become *the* star in a sport that was simply a hobby, not an industry, when he was born.

I had to visit him. I didn't know what to expect from staring at a burial plot, but I anticipated that I would be doing most of the talking.

I'm not sure what exactly pushed me towards this interest, but for years I've been captivated by Frank Russo's website thedeadballera.com. It chronicles the resting places of nearly every baseball player, umpire, owner and contributor in major league history. The first time I perused the site years ago, I spent hours reviewing the information, but felt that the author was somewhat creepy, twisted and morbid. I imagined someone who was teetering on the brink of insanity, continually questioning the fabric of our being and suffering from severe dementia. However, I came to find that Russo's work was more celebratory than twisted. It was just another avenue of baseball players' lives to explore, and I'm certainly not averse to discovery.

One of the first things that someone asks when he or she has heard a famous person has passed away is "how did it happen" or "how did they die?" Why would it be so different a quarter of a century later or 120 years later? Russo takes it a step further by visiting numerous ballplayers' gravesites and taking pictures to post on the website. I had never tried it and didn't know how I would feel going to a cemetery to visit the tombstone of someone who died more than 80 years before I was born. I thought there was no better place to start than with the memorable King Kelly.

Prior to leaving for Boston in early June, I mapped out the location of a handful of gravesites that I wished to visit, but was unsure if I would ever get to all of them. Russo warned that with lack of preparation you could wander around a cemetery aimlessly for hours and come up empty. Ill-preparedness is not a fault I possess. I double-checked the location of the cemetery in the southern suburbs of Boston, printed out directions from doorstep to cemetery gate to assure there would be no wrong turns, loaded the digital camera with new batteries, and wrote down the grave location with lane name, lot number, row number and exact plot.

Yet somehow I walked around that cemetery for over an hour.

Fresh off quadruple-checking the directions, mileage and grave location at my friend Emily's house, I departed for Mount Hope Cemetery in the early afternoon, expecting a 10-minute jaunt through the cemetery. When I drove through the gates, I immediately found myself on Walnut Avenue, the name of the road on which Kelly's burial site was located. It was a warm and humid day, probably in the mid-80s, and sweat trickled down my forehead while I sat in my car with the windows rolled up and the air conditioner off, fumbling about for my camera. The whisking breeze was pleasant as I opened the car door and stepped out, ready for a couple of quick camera shots and a moment of reflection. Kelly's spot was on Walnut Avenue, Lot 1650, Grave 21.

I immediately looked down and saw numbers in the 1900s, but those numbers dropped quickly so I expected to be very close. Instead of returning to the gates to gaze upon the cemetery map inside the Mount Hope offices, I felt I could stroll through the lots and find King Kelly.

After about 15 minutes of strolling, I was confused. Numbers were jumping all over the place. The lots numbered 1800 to 2100, so I crossed the road to find numbers ranging from 900 to 1300. The grass often consumed the lot numbers and many of the stones had settled deeper into the earth. A century's worth of weathering on the stones didn't make it easy to decipher the numbers either. Caretakers zipped around in other lots, assuming their grass cutting duties and regular maintenance, but I refused to ask for any help. I spent 30 more minutes wandering in and out of the rows of graves before I returned to my car. I maneuvered the car through the narrow lanes to find myself well beyond my desired location, overlooking a pond. This wasn't turning out to be as easy as I had hoped. My eagerness to find Kelly's gravesite was starting to do battle with my stubbornness and flat refusal to ask for help, creating an internal conflict that was, along with the heat of the afternoon, creating a new emotion: anger, edging towards rage.

I drove back to Walnut Avenue and ignored the side marked 1800-2100, having already examined it thoroughly. Back on the 900-1300 side, I began picking my way through the graves again, expecting to find something new. I realized I would never successfully navigate this labyrinth of graves without the aid of a map. I walked up to the cemetery offices, took two steps inside and found myself staring at a large map of the entire cemetery. Within about five seconds, I discovered my error. For some inexplicable reason, I dismissed a hill full of American flags on Walnut Avenue. It was just two weeks after Memorial Day and I concluded that these were American servicemen. Kelly's life spanned between the Civil War and the first World War, making it highly unlikely for his tombstone to earn a flag. Alas, Kelly was buried with his brethren of the Elks club of Boston, and apparently the organization simply filled their lots with flags.

Returning to the hill on Walnut Avenue, I quickly discovered Kelly's tombstone without the help of any cryptkeeping Sherpa. The stone was placed neatly near the top of the knoll next to other constituents belonging to the Benevolent and Protective Order of Elks and the grave received no special markings for it to stand out among the others. What struck me more than anything was the size of the grave. A lavish coffin or tombstone would have been expected for Kelly, who notoriously spent his wealth on clothing and other high-end products. That extravagance was deprived after Kelly's death as he was squeezed in with other members of his sect.

Now that I had found the grave, I wasn't really sure what to do. I never knew Kelly or had any real emotional attachment beyond my historical adoration, so I wasn't going to sit there and "talk" to him like a lost relative. As I stood there staring blankly at the name Michael Kelly, all I could think of was a century-old picture of Kelly with a full moustache, a drape-fitting uniform and a clever twinkle in his eye, conjuring a new scam to unleash upon an unsuspecting opponent.

Over the next week, I visited three other tombstones of former players that could not be more dissimilar. A day after seeing King Kelly, I stopped by the grave of Eddie Waitkus, who died of natural causes in the 1970s. Waitkus was the player who was shot by a deranged fan, inspiring the novel "The Natural" by Bernard Malamud. He was among row after row of World War II veterans, a chilling experience regardless of when and how the men died. Several days later, I revisited the King Kelly experience by circling a plot of land searching for Ray Chapman, who was universally adored by Cleveland Indians fans in the second decade of the 20th century. In mid-August 1920, a pitch from Carl Mays killed Chapman when the ball struck him in the temple. He failed to make it through the night despite heroic attempts by doctors to save the popular player's life. On a dismal rainy morning, I came across Chapman's large tombstone and accompanying sign. Even 86 years after his death, people honored their hero by leaning cracked baseball bats against the stone and dropping well-worn Cleveland hats at the foot of the tombstone. That same day, I journeyed to Ed Delahanty's final resting place. Big Ed remains the only player in major league history to win batting titles in both the American and National Leagues, but came to an untimely end in 1903 when he drowned near the Canadian border after being ejected from a train when he disturbed and threatened passengers while intoxicated. His was a family plot with a handful of baseball playing brothers accompanying him in eternal rest.

I'm not sure what I got out of visiting four gravesites of former ballplayers. There was some internal reflection, but I could have achieved that in virtually any cemetery. Perhaps it was just a matter of paying respect to men who were lucky enough to play baseball for a living. While I'm jealous of their talents, they likely would be jealous of me. I will never earn a paycheck for playing major league baseball, but I'll likely never have to witness the horrors of war and I probably will make it past the age of 36. That said, when I'm 80 years old, I wonder if I would want to trade my long life of ups and downs for the early grave that Mike Kelly earned from his frequents ups. My guess is that anyone nicknamed the King would probably invoke his no-trade clause.

Twice in a Lifetime

Several years ago, I convinced a pair of friends to sacrifice a week's vacation and travel around in the upper south for minor league baseball games. None of us knew what to expect. My friends, Dave and Ryan, looked upon the eight-day road trip as a vacation that happened to have some baseball games involved, enjoying the freedom away from their jobs with good food, golfing with friends, and plenty of alcohol. I viewed it as an opportunity to see some of the best players in the minor leagues in a short period of time. On consecutive days, I was able to watch Andy Marte, Miguel Cabrera and Jose Reyes, a trio of top prospects that were totally foreign names to my travel partners.

Over the course of the week, the three of us caught up on one another's lives and discussed the past and the future. There was only the occasional ripple of disagreement, and the stories brought back from the trip made it all worthwhile. We returned with new stories from each park thanks to Ryan, who is a gregarious type, as he made connections with locals in every ballpark we visited. The last game of the trip made for the best story, as Ryan befriended a middle-aged guy named Joe in Scranton, PA, at a Red Barons game. Through the extra-inning game, Dave, Ryan and Joe probably downed well over a case of beer and were shouting the praises of one Jason Knupfer, whose name was mispronounced repeatedly by Dave. He became so infatuated with him that he continually screamed, "I love Ka-nuff-er," amusing the entire section, though it began to wear on me by the 11th inning.

In October 2005, I tried to recapture the magic of that trip by planning another journey, this time to the Midwest. Ryan was quick to jump on the wagon again, but Dave begged off, explaining that he couldn't afford to take that kind of time off again with his new duties at work and the considerable expense. Though Ryan and I were disappointed that Dave would not be coming along, if for nothing more than the reduced financial commitment and Dave's unintentional comedy, we were both elated at the prospect of another trip. By the time June rolled around and all of the tickets were purchased, hotel rooms were reserved and the car was full of gas, the two of us were chomping at the bit to get back on the road. We would start our trek on a Thursday morning, driving westward from Boston to Erie, Pennsylvania.

Kids and Veterans

Eight-plus hours in a car isn't easy, especially on a beautiful day with nothing but sunshine and heat surrounding you. Ryan and I persevered, though he has the bladder of a 7-year-old girl. My policy in driving is to never stop unless the gas gauge is blinking empty or my bladder is about to explode. To ensure the latter does not occur, I refuse to drink anything until I am within 90 minutes of my destination or the gas stop. Ryan disregards these rules as foolhardy, which is why we stopped five or six times on the ride from Boston to Erie as he insisted on drinking several bottles of water. It mattered little, as we arrived in Erie well before game time and stopped at the hotel to drop off our luggage and rest for a few minutes.

The Erie Seawolves' Jerry Uht Park is one of my favorite stadiums in the minor leagues. There is virtually no foul ground, and it feels as if you could make a play in the game yourself if given the opportunity. Beyond the tall left field wall is the hockey arena, which also doubles as the clubhouses for the home and opposing teams, providing my favorite part of Jerry Uht Park. After batting practice the players all walk through the center field gate to retreat to the clubhouses to change for the game, only to re-emerge 20 minutes later. Since I had been to Erie before, I was aware of the center field entrance and decided to walk around the stadium to the players' parking lot to survey the scene.

Apparently I had misjudged the game time and arrived almost two hours before any real action would take place on the field, but my misstep turned into perfect timing. A local television crew was filming a puff piece, interviewing the ballplayers about their favorite baseball nuances, along with more frivolous questions with responses that required only one-word answers. Near the end of each interview, the attractive young woman would ask questions like "who is the best dancer" or "who is the biggest flirt" on the team. Admittedly, it was difficult to get the exact wording of the questions. I'm sure I could have made my way closer to eavesdrop, but I likely would have leaned into the camera's view. At least a dozen players fielded the questions with teammates standing around in their pre-game t-shirts and mesh shorts just listening and laughing, only to retreat to the locker room to retrieve another volunteer for the interviewer. Each and every time the players made it to the "who is the…" section, the answers would be the same and, as the questions progressed, the smiles on the players' faces would grow broader.

"Virgil Vasquez."

"Virgil Vasquez."

"Virgil Vasquez."

The answers even became comical to me, and all I knew about Virgil Vasquez was that he was a right-handed pitcher who was somewhat of a sleeper prospect as a 24-year-old in Double-A. It seemed as if old Virgil was a clubhouse favorite and quite the man about town.

The whole process was pleasing to see. While these young ballplayers are some of the most competitive athletes in the country, the game was still fun for them and the camaraderie was evident in their playful actions beyond that center field fence. Most of the players interviewed were still young, as only six players were born before the dawn of the 1980s, and several were only a year or two removed from college. In fact, right-handed pitcher Jair Jurrjens couldn't even get into the bar down the street legally, though I'm sure that the local establishments made some allowances for him and his teammates.

Ryan arrived mildly saturated after visiting one of those local establishments, explaining to me that some of the Erie boys had not behaved themselves over the course of the last few weeks. The owner of one of those nightclubs, located just a quarter of a mile down the road from the ballpark, overheard Ryan say to one of the waitresses that he was going to the game and that I knew some of the players on the team. There was a bit of a miscommunication there; I knew *of* the players on the team, I didn't actually *know* them. The owner told Ryan to make sure he and I brought the boys back down after the game and that all was forgiven. I never actually discovered what mischief occurred at the bar, but I could just imagine Tony Giarratano, a player who was drafted out of Tulane, getting into a little trouble. When your school is located in a city that is as notorious for partying as New Orleans, you just figure the guy with the $500,000 signing bonus *owns* the bar when he saunters in after a home game.

When the starting lineups were announced, I recognized most of the players, but one particular player caught my attention. Minor league veteran Gary Burnham made an appearance in the three-hole for the visiting Reading Phillies. I've seen Burnham play all over the International League and hardly expected him to be down in Double-A again. Burnham was drafted three times in the mid-1990s, once out of high school and twice while he was attending Clemson University. He finally signed in 1997 and played for the Phillies organization for five seasons before he was traded to the Toronto Blue Jays. It was with the Syracuse Sky Chiefs that I first met Burnham. In talking with him, I found Burnham to be a genuinely good person who not only excelled at playing baseball, but a guy who also tried his hand at drawing. His drawings still hang in the Sky Chiefs' gift shop for a couple of bucks apiece, though I think they are photocopies of the originals. I also recall a 16x20 color drawing of Pat Burrell, a former teammate of Burnham's in the Philadelphia system, which he completed.

I always stay unattached from teams and applaud only for players that I enjoy watching or players that I've met and found amiable. Gary Burnham is one of the great guys that I've had the pleasure of meeting and talking with in the minor leagues. Though I root for him as hard as any other minor leaguer, backing Burnham in his quest to reach the major leagues is the equivalent of betting the 100-to-1 shot at the race track because he has a pretty mane and a cool name. The likelihood of Burnham ever making it to the majors is remote at this point. At 31, he has played 10 years of minor league baseball, bouncing from organization to organization and competing in more ballparks than I'm sure he could even count. His career numbers are impressive (.294 batting average, 122 home runs, 636 runs batted in over the course of 1100 games), but his opportunities are becoming limited, revealed by the fact that he spent 2005 in the independent Atlantic League. He is now at the age where he is a minor league free agent virtually every season, able to make a considerably higher wage than the normal minor league stipend. But even with his increased salary, money is tight for a ballplayer gainfully employed for only six months. I remember a friend of mine remarking about his artwork late in the 2003 season and Burnham responded, "You should go buy some; I depend on it." Apparently the minor league free-agent market was not making Burnham a rich man.

That's the way it is in the upper minor leagues through Double-A and Triple-A. Many of the players are termed "organizational players," serving basically as fillers for the rosters. Those players help provide the product on the field at the local level and are usually the ones that win championships since the younger prospects are still learning the game or move to the majors too quickly to make much of a lasting impact on the local minor league team. Burnham probably once was like Tony Giarratano, Jair Jurrjens and Virgil Vasquez, just a kid playing the game and getting paid for it, full of major league dreams. It's likely at least one of those prospects will be bumming around Erie or some other Eastern League city five or six years from now, unready to ease into real life.

When the game was over, a 5-4 Erie victory, Burnham was one of the last players to leave the sanctity of the visiting team's dugout. He took two steps out of the dugout and came directly over to the railing, close to where I was seated. His hands full, he dropped his glove and some other personal items and took time to talk to the fans and sign some autographs. He then completed his post-game philanthropy by handing his bat to a 10-year-old kid in the stands. I wished that some of those free-spirited players who were laughing outside the center field fence in pre-game had been there to see Burnham, who was one of the last two players to exit the field. They could have seen an athlete near the end of his career handle himself with class and dignity, learning the way both a player and a man should act.

Are You Guys Married?

Stop me if you've heard this before: I hate showing up to games late and I despise unexpected traffic or roadwork.

Both Ryan and I were already in an awful mood when we reached our hotel in Kalamazoo, Michigan, after six hours in the car. Driving into Kalamazoo wasn't the most pleasant experience, as the sky was gray with a sickly smog rather than clouds, though I'm not sure the small city even has smog, and the locals seemed unfriendly. Our accommodations were atrocious and we both joked about how many shots we would need upon returning home. Just sitting down on the bedspread made me feel as though I contracted a flesh-eating bacterium. We concluded that the less time spent in this hotel, the fewer vaccinations we would need. It took about 20 seconds for us to drop off our bags and bolt out the back door. It was vital to move quickly so as to not gag on the noxious fumes, which bordered on mustard gas, emanating in the hallway. I'm not kidding. It smelled like some sort of hybridization of flatulence and spoiled eggs covered in mustard.

Turning on to the highway, I was immediately met by my archenemy and recurring nemesis: yellow and orange blinking signs indicating road construction. Over the next 15 minutes, Ryan and I traveled about two miles, before being met by a series of streetlights set approximately ten feet apart. Searching for a viable restaurant took another 20 minutes and my rage was consuming me so much that I began spitting out a stream of unintelligible obscenities like the father in the movie *A Christmas Story*. I very well might have muttered "naddafinga" in my tantrum. A slight misty rain began to fall as we pulled into a random restaurant, something I noticed more than the car I nearly ran into. Ryan was glad to get out of the car.

As a souvenir of survival, I took a business card of the restaurant, The Craftsman Chop Company, which was actually located in nearby Portage. Printed on the card, below the company logo, were the words "eat, drink, relax." Those words and the kindly waitress behind the bar worked as some sort of hypnosis, because I did just that. After a 40-minute meal, Ryan and I exited the eatery feeling much better and hopped back in the car as the sun began to peak through the clouds. It was as if The Craftsman Chop Company willed the clouds to scatter and make my day in Michigan better. I am forever grateful. Otherwise I might still be awaiting a trial date in Kalamazoo County.

We still had another 60 miles to drive to get to Fifth Third Ballpark just north of Grand Rapids, but the meal had me revitalized and I was prepared to hit the gas pedal. Zooming through the southern suburbs, we hit traffic again, but I did not panic this time around. Fortunately, a sign a few miles back warned of a traffic accident and I was wary to avoid it. Ducking off an unknown exit several miles south of our destination, I somehow expertly navigated the city's side streets and made my way north, just a quarter of a mile from the stadium. Ryan was baffled at how I meandered my way through this unknown city by glancing at a microscopic map in my atlas while dodging rush hour traffic.

Fifth Third Ballpark stood like an oasis off the highway with lines of cars awaiting admittance to the parking lot. The scene resembled a circus atmosphere of which I had never seen for a regular season game, coming closer to the appearance of a spring training facility than a Low-A Midwest League ballpark. It was easy to see how the West Michigan Whitecaps regularly ranked near the top of the attendance figures among all five full-season Class-A leagues. With a significant population from which to draw, a beautiful park and a history of winning in the dozen years that the team had operated in the northern suburbs of Grand Rapids, attracting fans was effortless. The publication *Baseball America* even named the team the Class-A

Organization of the Decade for the 1990s and the club certainly looks to have a head start for the first decade of the 21st century, too. With stud Cameron Maybin, one of the top young players in all of the minor leagues, roaming the outfield and impressing fans with his five-tool* talent package, the 2006 West Michigan Whitecaps' season was complete with everything a minor league fan could possibly want.

Even with all of the positives, it didn't mean that the Whitecaps stopped trying to bring in fans. A yearly event, I was told, took place on the field for pre-game as an elephant threw out the ceremonial first pitch. Yeah, an elephant. The animal threw absolute gas, too, as the pitch looked like it reached the plate with velocity in the mid-60s. I'm hoping this breaks down further barriers and someday an anteater toes the rubber to snort out a strike.

By the time Ryan and I took our seats, the sun was out in full force and the humidity added from the passing storm made the close quarters uncomfortable. While I like a full park for the added enthusiasm of the local fans, I also like a little space so I don't pass out from the heat. Luckily for Ryan and me, our seat neighbors made the game even more pleasurable. I never caught the names of the pair of West Michigan enthusiasts, a man in his early-40s and his 10-year-old son, but the father struck up a conversation with Ryan, who was more than willing to expound upon the details of our trip. The father was enthralled and peppered us both with questions for the final five innings of the contest. Usually I wouldn't be happy with the constant barrage, but his interjections made the conversation genuinely interesting, save for one confusing question.

---

* For those unfamiliar with the baseball terminology, a "tool" is scouting lingo for the measurement of a certain ability in one area of the game. To be a "five-tool" player, means that the ballplayer has average or better ability in the following categories: running, throwing, fielding, hitting and hitting for power. Though the term is tossed around frequently in baseball circles, there are very few true five-tool players in the major leagues. At the beginning of his career, Alex Rodriguez was a prime example of a five-tool player.

"Are you guys married?"

Ryan and I were both taken aback.

"No!" we fired back simultaneously.

Ryan was my college roommate in my senior year and I again lived with him for a year in Boston and have kept in close contact since departing Massachusetts, visiting Beantown at least a couple times per year in all seasons to catch up with him and a host of other friends. We are tight friends, but our discussions can sometimes mimic an old married couple arguing over the simplest of topics. I often rein him in on matters like drinking, finances and other sensible things, while he is equally capable of keeping me on task when I get fired up over the little things, allowing me to focus and understand the big picture. That said, we are both stringent heterosexuals and were a bit unsure of where this guy was going with his question. Not that there is anything wrong with it.

"Um, no, if we were married with kids or something, we couldn't leave the house for long trips and travel around to see games," I responded, obviously unnerved.

"If I was married, I could never get to spend this much money or anything," Ryan added. "In fact, my girlfriend has been checking in on me every couple hours."

"Yeah, she calls like three or four times a day, at least." I was going to make sure that no matter how progressive and tolerant this guy might be, he was going to *know* that Ryan and I were not gay.

What is it about the heterosexual male that causes them to be so standoffish about homosexuality? I seriously doubt that when a homosexual male is accused of being straight, he doesn't immediately retreat to some flamboyant defense mechanism to prove his gayness. Our responses were ridiculous, but it didn't matter because Ryan and I spent the next 10 minutes dropping unsubtle hints that we both loved women. If the opportunity presented itself, I'm sure either one of us would have been happy to have intercourse with one of the girls walking up and down the aisles selling peanuts. Maybe even broadcast it on the giant scoreboard to make sure everyone in the stadium knew.

Once Ryan and I regained our senses after our homophobic lunacy, the conversation returned to the subject of baseball and the older gentlemen stuck around after the game to talk more about his own movements in the professional baseball world. As a military man, he had been stationed all over the country and watched games from New Mexico to South Carolina. Listening to him go on and on about the past, I noticed that he was becoming more energized with every retold story. Our trip was reminding him of his past and the freedoms he enjoyed as a young man before the inevitable reached out and grabbed him: that troubling thing known as responsibility. He admitted that he was jealous of our trip, but wouldn't trade his current standing for anything, looking down at his respectful son who had stood there speechless for a quarter of an hour. Seeing his son's dutiful patience was running thin, the man bid us farewell and shook our hands heartily, wishing us luck on the remainder of the road trip. His hand instinctively went to his son's back in a manner of leading and protection, but he also looked back and waved a final time.

It was a perfect adieu. He may have been envious of Ryan and me, but he was a step ahead of us, watching a ballgame with his son. I bet any remnants of jealousy truly melted away the very next time he played catch with his boy in the backyard.

Watch Out for the Hitman

Many years ago, George Carlin contrasted the two most popular sports in the United States, baseball and football, with his brilliant comedic writing and timing. I've listened to the bit and read the text numerous times and have trouble deciding if Carlin prefers one to the other because he mocks the terminology of both so brilliantly. When you think about the differences between the two sports, it really is amazing that someone could be heart-committed to both. I used to be one of those people, and if you threw in basketball, the lines of preference became even murkier. Over time, my interest in professional basketball waned to its current point of indifference, while it took longer for professional football to drop off the map, though I do still occasionally watch NFL games. I still love college basketball, but never could get into college football.

When I told friends and acquaintances of my trip to the Midwest for ballgames and mentioned South Bend, people immediately thought that I was visiting the University of Notre Dame. Funny, I immediately thought of the Midwest League's South Bend Silverhawks, complete with stud outfielder Justin Upton, and never thought of stopping by the hallowed ground of college football's past. It sounded like a nice addition to the journey and walking around the campus would be a pleasant alternative to the sessile lifestyle I had taken to as a barnacle to my car's driver seat in the past few days.

Driving on to the Notre Dame campus was somewhat surreal as we rolled further into the land of the Fighting Irish, the sun dancing

74

off the cathedral of the admissions building at the end of the long entrance road. After finding an appropriate parking spot, Ryan and I were astonished by the grass. Not the grassy turf inside a stadium or in an expertly manicured garden, but the lawn underneath our feet as we walked from building to building. After a brief time, I wondered aloud if it was permissible to walk on the grass and questioned whether the two of us had violated some time-honored sacred tradition of using only sidewalks. The grass was that flawless. My guess is that Notre Dame receives a fair amount of donations and sometimes spreads the monetary contributions to campus upkeep above and beyond the norm.

A few college students walked across the grass from one building to the next, assuring me that campus safety would not be imminently arriving to bash our heads in for our gross misconduct. Breathing dual sighs of relief, Ryan and I headed to the Joyce Center gift shop to purchase souvenirs. My selection was for my friend Pittsy, who occasionally reaches catatonic states when discussing or viewing Notre Dame football, while Ryan wanted something more visceral. He purchased a rubber football covered with the Fighting Irish logo and suggested we hurl the faux pigskin back and forth on the lawn.

Not having tossed a football in quite some time, I relearned how to throw a football correctly so it would spiral and travel more than 25 yards at a time while Ryan adeptly ran passing patterns in the thick grass beneath our feet. I astutely let Ryan run the passing routes and made my throws from underneath a large tree since the temperature was easing its way past 90 degrees. The whole process of throwing a ball around on the Notre Dame campus was somewhat dreamy. It's been more than 20 years since I attended my first professional baseball game and can recall numerous details. I wondered if kids who adored football felt the same glee when first arriving to Notre Dame Stadium. I soon discovered that even vicarious glee could provide for odd reactions.

Ryan halted our play for a few moments to visit a restroom, so I decided to call Pittsy and tell him where I was. He seemed to be swept into a bit of a frenzy when I told him of our exact location and activity, even going so far as to reveal that he was now sexually excited. Recalling the uncomfortable conversation at Fifth Third Ballpark the night before, I told Pittsy I was glad that he was a thousand miles away and that he needed to locate his fiancé.

Religious statues litter the Notre Dame campus and just to the side of the tree from which I had been throwing the football was a seated Jesus Christ with his hand out. I'm sure it was significant of something, but Ryan and I both noticed that the statue's right hand was out with its first two fingers extended outward. We immediately concluded two things: first, that Jesus was providing sinners a proctology examination (one would think that holy omniscience would suffice), and second, that we were both going to hell much faster than either of us ever thought possible. In fact, both of us felt it to be a good time to exit the Notre Dame campus before an otherwise sunny day was suddenly filled with thunderstorms and bolts of lightning aimed at our hides.

When we pulled into the parking lot of Coveleski Regional Stadium, I felt I was more at home. Stadiums like Fifth Third Ballpark in Grand Rapids, Michigan, are great and probably offer more to the average fan, but I prefer insouciant venues with characteristics that are thought provoking rather than those which are shoved in the faces of the patrons. Unfortunately, that is not what the average fan wants and Coveleski Regional is stuck in the middle, much the same way that the Sky Dome/Rogers Centre is in Toronto. The parks aren't old enough to be classic and not new enough to be considered neo-retro, dooming them to perceived inadequacies despite the numerous amenities that make them viable to their communities.

Of course, if you have Justin Upton playing center field, you shouldn't need amenities.

Upton was the first round draft choice of the Arizona Diamondbacks in 2005, the first selection overall, and probably one of the most ballyhooed high school prospects of the past 25 years, especially considering his lineage to older brother Melvin (BJ), the second-overall pick of the 2002 MLB draft. Justin Upton is one of the most talented players I've ever seen. It was easy to pick him out even in warm ups by simply watching him run, throw and swing a bat gracefully in the outfield grass. For years I had followed his progression through the high school ranks and the numerous showcases that he attended with scouts drooling over his skill set. I read about major league bat speed and world-class 60-yard dash times, one registering at 6.24 seconds. Prior to the game even beginning, those tools were easy to notice. A line of autograph seekers set up across the rail, hoping that the rising star would stop to sign.

Once the game began, Upton again flashed his impressive tools, calmly trotting to three fly balls in center field and snaring them with ease before jogging back in to the dugout. Numerous times I tried to snap a picture of him, but my digital camera was beginning its dysfunctional path towards oblivion. My mind's eye would have to recall the movements of the great young Upton in both the field and at the plate, where he would complete a 1-for-3 day with a run driven in.

Upton was originally the player that I wanted to maintain focus on throughout the game, but when the starting lineups were announced, fear struck at my heart and my body clenched up with my eyes darting about. The opposing Lansing Lugnuts were employing a young outfielder by the name of Cory Patton, and I knew nothing good could come of this fact. I was correct to surmise as much.

While standing in the on-deck circle before his third inning at bat, Patton must have caught me out of the corner of his eye, deciding then and there to finish the job. There is a chance that Patton is attempting to fulfill a contract through the mob, hoping to end my life for whatever reason. I'll pay him double if he just leaves me alone.

Back in 2005, when Patton was playing for the Auburn Doubledays as a 6th round pick of the Toronto Blue Jays from the previous year, he ripped a screaming foul ball at me that I barely avoided as if I was Neo dodging bullets on the rooftop in the movie *The Matrix*. On another occasion he hit a looping pop fly that bounced one seat in front of me and nearly took my head off on the ricochet when the woman in front misplayed the easy catch. I've since come to believe she was an accomplice.

Now, sitting just a half-dozen rows up on the first base side at Coveleski Regional Stadium in South Bend, Indiana, hundreds of miles from our first two encounters, I was once again unprotected by a screen or a low wall. The first two batters struck out to start the inning when Patton approached the plate, his gaze bouncing between the ground, the batter's box and the crowd behind the first base dugout. With every waggle of the bat in the left-handed hitting side of the batter's box, his right eye's peripheral vision must have been catching my location, assuring him of the appropriate mark. A vicious cut and not enough pine tar sent the bat out of his hands and hurtling through the air, "accidentally" in my direction. Impulsively, I put my hands up to nab the bat out of its flight and I could feel the change in wind current as it passed over my outstretched fingers, careening off seats and bounding several times into the general admission sections. If I had been standing up, Patton's hurled lumber likely would have caught me anywhere between the upper chest and forehead. For a third time I had come out of a Cory Patton encounter unscathed, but a part of me is praying for him to stick in the low minors because I see an awful lot of games in New Hampshire and Syracuse. I would rather not give him any more opportunities to carry out his evil plans.

Opium Den: Exit Six Miles

And I thought the first sign was comical.

While driving through Chicago Sunday morning, a blinking road sign revealed this startling and enigmatic truth: Avoid The Ryan. Sure, this was just a way of telling motorists to stay away from the Dan Ryan Expressway to avoid traffic congestion, but it reminded me of some sort of Chinese Zodiac placemat in a buffet restaurant telling me that my opposite is the wolf and I'm compatible with the lizard. I remarked to my travel partner that he was lucky that he didn't live in Chicago with a sign dangling from his neck to warn all women to "Avoid The Ryan." While the two of us chuckled about the ramifications of the traffic sign and Ryan trying to find love in Chicago, it would not come close to the sign situated across the state line in Wisconsin. Unaware that such a road sign could possibly exist, we wiped our eyes, shook our heads, and then wiped our eyes again in disbelief at this placard: Bong Recreation Area.

Had we missed something? Were narcotics legal in Wisconsin? Had laws been passed over the last week? I expected oddly-named stores lining the roadside selling drug paraphernalia, black lights, tie-dyed shirts and bottles of patchouli perfume with hippies singing at the store front while vans resembling the "Mystery Machine" rocked back and forth in the name of free love. Disappointed, we drove the next few miles with no further mention of the Bong Recreation Area, and I became to think that perhaps we had been hallucinating in the midst of a pelting rain.

I later discovered, thanks to a resident of Wisconsin, the Bong Recreation Area is named after Richard Ira Bong, a World War II flying ace who shot down 40 Japanese planes in the Pacific. Ironically, despite making it through two years of combat unharmed, Bong was killed in his routine work as a test pilot when his Lockheed P-80 Shooting Star malfunctioned. He bailed out successfully, but the malfunction took place before the plane could reach a sufficient height for an acceptable ejection. Coincidentally, the accident took place on the same day that the United States dropped the first atomic bob on Hiroshima.

It's insulting to mock the dead, especially when they are American heroes, but are you telling me the Wisconsin Legislature or whoever is in charge of these things didn't have the foresight or at least the good sense to change the sign to the "Richard Bong Recreation Area?" Maybe this is the state's way of making people look up information regarding Mr. Bong so that his exploits will be remembered forever.

Torrential rains dropped from the sky as we closed in on Milwaukee, but I recalled that Miller Park used a retractable roof for such occasions and sailed on into the city without fear of a cancellation. Another recollection which sprung to mind was that a few years ago Milwaukee ranked among the fattest cities in the country, but supposedly the city was now positioned among the fittest cities in the country. From what I saw in the stadium's parking lot, the letter "i" in fittest was clearly a typo. The city might lead the country in open-heart and gastric bypass surgeries, but the people I saw clearly did not weigh in with their votes during the more recently published exercise poll. Ninety minutes before game time, despite the rain still drizzling, Brewers fans lined the parking lots with grills and coolers, sipping suds and downing brats at an artery-clogging pace. I loosened my belt just watching the display. In each direction I saw people double-fisting, sometimes with beer, sometimes with bratwurst, but mostly with one of each, and the only thing any of these people used resembling a treadmill was an escalator to the second floor of the food court. I've been to a lot of games and I've witnessed tailgating before, but these Milwaukee fans were professionals and almost made it appear artistic, majestically posing like Greek statues with heads held upward holding a beer in one hand and a brat in the other. Football is notorious for tailgating since it lends itself to debauchery and the condemnation of moral acts, but baseball is family bonding time, and that couldn't be any more clear since this Sunday was Father's Day.* Regardless, the tailgaters were out in full force on this dreary Sunday, splitting their collective Wisconsin allegiance by sporting jerseys of either the Milwaukee Brewers or the Green Bay Packers' Brett Favre, usually in size XXXL.

Fat camp opposition continued once inside Miller Park. During the game, Ryan and I figured that the beer guys outnumbered all other concession workers by a ratio of approximately 10-to-1. How could anyone leave this park standing upright? It was nearly impossible to leave sober with beer pushers running up and down the aisles every two minutes. Ryan worked his way through five beers in three innings and came to the conclusion he needed to slow down. The same could have been said for me. With my pants already loosened from the parking lot imagery, I had already downed two brats and was eyeing a third. If fans driving home could somehow navigate the roads in a drunken haze and survive, they certainly could not avoid the slow death of congestive heart failure by age 50.

Along with this Sunday being a holiday, the Brewers played the day in retro-style, wearing the pinstriped jerseys (I've read that pinstripes on clothing, much like black, provide the wearer the illusion of a thinner frame) from the glory days of Milwaukee. The team even brought back the immortal Jerry Augustine for an appearance. Augustine had spent the past 12 seasons at the University of

---

* *I would just like to note that the combination of baseball and Father's Day reminds me one of the funniest lines I've ever heard uttered from a broadcast booth. Ralph Kiner, during a Mets' game, once proclaimed, "Today is Father's Day, so to all you fathers out there, Happy Birthday!" I nearly choked with laughter.*

Wisconsin-Milwaukee as the school's head baseball coach only to step down at the conclusion of the 2006 season to focus on his insurance business. He was scheduled to sign autographs for Brewers fans during the game and a lengthy line accumulated an hour before his arrival, which came as a surprise to me. Jerry Augustine won 55 games and lost 59 in his modest 10-year career, winning 43 of those games in a four-year stretch from 1976-79 (he also ranked among the American League leaders with 18 losses in 1977). His 10-year career was actually closer to eight seasons since he pitched in 26 innings in September 1975 and only five innings in April 1984. Yet somehow, Jerry Augustine touched the lives of these fans in a way I couldn't understand. It was equivalent to a large company welcoming back a faceless drone who worked in a cubicle for eight years with an afternoon picnic and softball game celebrating the glorious return. If the Milwaukee fans could get this excited over Jerry Augustine, imagine the community's reaction to free angioplasty day.

A few innings into the contest, Ryan and I became distraught with the fragile pitching of Zach Jackson, who was struggling mightily with his control and made the sticky stadium even more uncomfortable. Three innings of slapping thighs with our neighbors became too much and Ryan hopped the seat behind him to sit in a better ventilated row. A half inning later, I joined him and was pleased to find an unreserved older gentleman sitting directly behind us. The banter in which he and his son reveled was pure joy. Barking back at one another lovingly at a baseball game came as a delightful and unexpected bonus to our relocation, especially when the old man threw in an *Austin Powers* moment when he reiterated that he didn't speak any "hutchy-stutchy Polish." Neither Ryan nor I could successfully decipher "hutchy-stutchy," but its similarities to Dr. Evil's "freaky-deaky Dutch" gave me a fairly clear idea of what the old cogger was trying to say.

Over 43,000 fans stuck around to watch Milwaukee closer Derrick Turnbow strike out the side in the top of the ninth and then get credited with the victory when Carlos Lee hit a walk-off, three-run home run in the bottom of the inning, but Ryan and I did not witness either occurrence inside the stadium since we left after the eighth inning. While the old man entertained us for a few more innings, especially when we engaged him in conversation, neither of us could take the sights and smells of the ballpark for much longer. Ryan was half in the bag from numerous helpings of beer, and the brats sat in my stomach like lumps of cement. Clearly we were amateurs in the world of tailgating and we hadn't even sat outside in the rain consuming a pre-game meal. Four hours back to the hotel in South Bend couldn't come fast enough, but at least our early departure prevented us from seeing much traffic and the inclement weather was now just a postscript to the journey.

If only such afterthoughts were available for the small town of Hartford, Wisconsin. Located just 30 miles to the northwest of Milwaukee, Hartford had a tornado rip through its community which caused wide spread damage, but fortunately the twister inflicted no serious injuries. Apparently, several other funnel clouds had appeared in the storm system through which we had driven on the way to Milwaukee.

To me, there was only one possible conclusion: it was an atmospheric anomaly caused by a collective exhalation by those at the Bong Recreation Area.

Getting a Snoot Full

A popular belief in every ballpark across the country is that the real fans sit in the bleachers. Sit in the bleachers for a ballgame and, supposedly, you will discover brilliant baseball minds who live and die with every pitch along with characters that achieve local prominence for equal parts wackiness and due diligence. The only reason that these fans choose to watch the game from the bleachers is that they are baseball purists, not that they lack the financial means to sit close to the action and savor the game's nuances from a prime location.

Truth be known, these people aren't the brilliant minded, rah-rah cheerleaders they are made out to be by writers and television announcers. The reason they don't sit close to the action isn't because they don't want to appear as sellouts. It's because they can't afford the tickets. The bleachers are the beer-swilling, potty-mouthed, gluttonous, poor white-trash section of ballparks.

So I bought tickets for the bleachers at Jacobs Field in Cleveland, Ohio.

It seemed safe enough. You watch the movie *Major League* and its just a couple guys in native headdresses banging a drum while arguing about the trajectory of a home run. Of course that movie was shot when the team was still playing in Cleveland Municipal Stadium, a few seasons before Jacobs Field opened, so things might have changed when the team moved.

The first time I went to Jacobs Field, I felt cheated. Attending a game with three friends in the club seats where food was free (along with the tickets, thanks to one of the friends who worked at a local radio station) and handed out by numerous attendants, we came only 20 minutes before the game began because of some tardiness by my friends.

I always want to arrive early for games, but at major league games it is much more vital because the area to explore is so much larger. This time, only a heavy rain prevented an early arrival. The gates swung open 90 minutes prior to game time and I traversed the concourse, discovering the ballpark's fare and circus-like booths. I signed up for a credit card at one of the MasterCard stations that seem to be located in each major league and upper minor league ballpark across the country. The most important part was the free Indians t-shirt. It was imperative that I fit in among the clique in the outfield stands.

Already up a free souvenir for the day, I gleefully pulled the t-shirt over the top of my other shirt to proudly display my affinity for Cleveland on this day. A toothy grin smiled from the logo on my shirt at all of the people I passed as I made my way towards my seat halfway up the bleachers. Only a few fans were scattered throughout the outfield sections so far, but it would gradually change as the opposing Cubs fans began to litter the seats in front of us. Obnoxious and loathsome, the clan of Cubbie supporters was almost viral, appearing to gain in strength and volume as game time grew near. With the opposition louder than the home team's fans, the Indians' corps refused to be outdone.

"The Cubs are going to take it in the ass!" shouted the girl sitting next to me. The shriek was piercing and brought about an unintelligible response from the throng of Cubs fans. I'm all for heckling, but only if it's original. Cubs taking it in the ass ranks right up there as an equivalent for those on sports talk radio that simply yell louder to get their point across. It doesn't make it right, and all it does is irritate everyone else. At least the girl was sort of cute. Not really. Remember, I'd been sitting next to Ryan for four straight days.

The girl and her friend were somewhat attractive but dated, with early 90s haircuts and clothing, so the bleachers were likely a regular home for them. The gross negligence of fashion trends didn't stop Ryan and me from flirting with them for 10 minutes. It appeared as if Ryan would have a pair of drinking partners for this game, something he sorely had missed since the days of 2003 with Dave, Scranton Joe, and the batting of Jason Knupfer. I was happy for him.

"We're gonna go get more beer so save our seats," the slightly plump brunette said to me. I nodded, not really caring that much if they came back at all. Five minutes later, four Detroit Tigers fans sat down, sending Ryan and me to our assigned seats two spots down. Leaning to my right, I nudged Ryan, "Why do I think those girls are going to be pissed when they get back?"

Two minutes later, the girls rained down a storm of inappropriate language upon me as they stumbled through people enjoying the game. Sitting diagonally to Ryan and me, I was referred to, on a number of occasions, as an asshole, which was fine by me since I was at the game to watch some baseball, not for a one-night stand with a skank from Shaker Heights. Ryan smoothed things over with the ladies and continued his discussion, though he was miffed the girls did not return with beer for him or me, a point he brought up regarding the seat saving.

The outfield stands were now filled with an eclectic group of watchers, wearing every regional baseball logo imaginable. Cubs and Indians were at the forefront, but the Tigers were well represented, and booed, as were the Cincinnati Reds and Pittsburgh Pirates. A lone Chicago White Sox fan stood up in the second inning to proudly show his jersey, backing the 2005 World Series Champion, but his posturing was quickly deflated when the Cubs fans made it known that no one in *Chicago* even cared about the White Sox.

Some time in the fourth inning, I got up to use the restroom, and the girls, unready to let the past be the past, informed me that my seat would be taken when I returned. I smirked and made my way down the concrete steps to the hallway, deciding that I would leave Ryan for a few innings and watch the game from the Home Run Porch adjacent to the bleachers. Unfortunately, I just could not escape the idiocy of the Cubs fans, as some guy was walking around in a Mark Prior jersey. That support was fine, but he accompanied the jersey with face painting, blue Christmas garland draped over his neck like an anaconda, and incoherent screaming that reminded me of a schizophrenic off his medication.

Call me boring, but I just don't get it. In a college atmosphere, I can understand the allure of acting like an idiot. Those are still formative years where everyone is still trying to find an identity, and experimentation with creative and mildly unruly behavior is an effective outlet for the stress and pressure felt by students, along with binge drinking. At professional sporting events, however, I cannot surmise what the thought process is for outlandish behavior and dress that borders on odd fetishes and mental disorders. Being whipped into a frenzy by a sporting event is a primal reaction that society should outgrow. The mob mentality and riots caused by soccer in Europe and other football-crazed countries across the world should provide a model to *not* follow; yet the fans in the United States choose to emulate the insanity and revel in the debauchery. I suppose I'm in the minority since every time I watch an NFL game the camera zooms in on some nut wearing spiked shoulder pads or a guy wearing a dress and a false pig nose.

All of that preparation by the Cubs fans mattered little since another heavy rain loaded with thunder and bolts of lightning came and washed out the next hour of our lives. Tired and cramped by maniacs in the shelter of the concourse, Ryan and I fled Jacobs Field for food and the comfort of the hotel. He sought sleep and rest. My only desire was to escape the ward and embrace a return to normalcy.

Amateur Night

Following a 16-hour driving excursion that brought me from Cleveland to Boston and back to northern New York, I decided to return to my roots with a game in Ottawa. Sure, I've been there 50 times and have written about it to death already, but I just can't help it. The city and park keep delivering stories more interesting than any other stadium. The most decorated team in the International League, the Durham Bulls, began a four-game series against the Lynx on June 22nd and the situation was full of possibilities. The team is just loaded with future stars. Or are the future stars just loaded?

Elijah Dukes, BJ Upton and Delmon Young are three of the most gifted athletes in minor league baseball. Unfortunately, they also share another title to go along with professional baseball player: fodder for the public blotter.

Dukes is characterized by the minor league media as a borderline sociopath as he continues to have run-ins with everyone from umpires to opponents to his own coaching staff. I was disappointed to discover that he did not make the trip to Ottawa because he was serving a team suspension, believed to be a problem with hitting coach Richie Hebner. I've never met him personally, so I don't know what kind of person he is, but from everything I've read, it sounds as if he is a very confused and volatile young man.

Upton was once considered in the conversation for best prospect in baseball, along with Twins catcher Joe Mauer, during the 2003 and 2004 seasons. He had incredible pressure placed upon him as he signed for well over four million dollars back in 2002 as the second overall pick of the draft. He moved so quickly through the minors that, after not playing a single professional game in 2002, he was in the major leagues by August 2004, just a few weeks shy of his 20th birthday. While his offense is undeniably major-league ready, his ability to play shortstop is constantly being scrutinized by scouts. It isn't a lack of talent, because he can certainly compete at the position with his range and athleticism. The problem lies in all of the throws he makes that nearly decapitate people in the first few rows of the box seats that have scouts questioning him. Upton has been uninterested in moving positions because he really does want to play shortstop. You can't blame the young man for taking on the challenge, but it is probably in the Devil Rays best interest to move him to the outfield or to second base, where he would probably produce at levels similar to Alfonso Soriano. While he normally has been a model citizen, he was arrested the previous weekend for driving while under the influence. It made me wonder whether or not he would be permitted to enter Canada. Though the charge is on the record, the conviction is not, so he played.

Young, one of the most hyped outfield prospects of the last decade who boldly claimed after he was drafted that he would be in the big leagues within a year, recently finished his 50-game suspension for tossing a bat at a replacement umpire in late-April. This was his first road trip after the conclusion of the suspension, and Ottawa was the best place he could possibly go to after such an incident. There is virtually no pressure and no catcalling in Ottawa. During warm ups, a couple of idiot fans did make some comments about him throwing bats, but they were so unoriginal and preconceived that it was hard to take them seriously.

The comments made me wonder behind what corner my "friend" from Montreal, the Caucasian Grimace, was hiding. Delmon Young would be like Christmas and New Year's wrapped into one for the Caucasian Grimace. It was not meant to be. Apparently, the Lynx decided to revoke his season tickets following the Ruben Rivera incident. That news absolutely thrilled me, but a part of me wanted to see if Delmon Young would bounce Caucasian Grimace's head off the top of the dugout. Knowing Young, I'm fairly sure he would have ignored the heckler; but as proven by his 50-game suspension, he has showed that he sometimes expresses his anger in a variety of ways.

This game looked as if it could be a blast with all of the future stars on the field. I was able to procure four autographs of Young with the help of a couple friends, and I even landed a signature from the mercurial Upton, who looked as if he was being told that dinner would be nothing but Brussels sprouts, once. With such a haul, I was in a great mood for the game.

And then amateur night began.

A middle-aged women's softball team came marching in, 20 strong, and sat in the row directly behind me, about a dozen rows up beyond the first base dugout. They had arrived on a bus just as the first pitch was being thrown, with one of them decorated in a white veil and gloves. Already drunk, the bachelorette party was ready to enjoy an evening of decadence at the ballpark. It all started out harmless enough. A few calls here and there to the players as they checked out the athletic meat on the field. However, in the second inning they found their target for the evening, Durham catcher Shawn Riggans.

Riggans is a 25-year-old catcher, a solid prospect who has sustained several injuries over the years that have held him back. He has never amassed 400 plate appearances in a season and peaked at 313 at bats in 2005. As the bellows from the horny first wives' club came from above, I thought to myself, hasn't he suffered enough?

But Riggans played along well. In the bottom of the third inning, the ladies started calling to Upton to have Riggans come out of the dugout so they could check him out some more. With the quick conclusion to the inning, Riggans obliged by running his 6-2 athletic frame to his spot behind the plate. Several of the girls called to him by screaming his name and a few other mostly appropriate comments. He smiled sheepishly and the women went wild with a few more calls, which he responded to with a fist pump. While on-deck the following inning, the ladies came out with, "Nice buns there, 25," and again Riggans acknowledged with an extended right hand. Just an inning later, Riggans was back behind the plate, but a 58-foot pitch bounced up and caught him square in the cup, knocking the wind out of him for a moment.

"Tara, he's no good any more," one screamed to another.

The show was mildly amusing, much like watching a Gallagher comedy show when you aren't in the front row and he's smashing watermelons with a giant mallet. It was at that moment that one of the ushers at the Gallagher show tapped me on the shoulder and said I should be in the front row. In other words, the girls decided it was time for me to be involved with their performance.

"Hey, Mr. Scorekeeper," Tara said.

I ignored.

"Hey, Mr. Scorekeeper," Tara repeated so that everyone within three sections could hear. Okay, I had to have heard that one.

"Yes?"

"Can I keep score for an inning?"

"Sorry, I don't let anyone else keep score for me during the game,"

"No, it's okay. I know how to do it."

"I'm sure you do, but I don't like anyone else to write in my book,"

"Come on. We'll trade! I'll keep score and you can drink beer!"

As intriguing as that did sound, I was reluctant to let Tara keep my scorebook. She was probably only an inning away from refunding some of the beer and it wasn't going to be on my scorebook. I was able to fend her off with some excuses of why I couldn't drink beer or let her anywhere near my scorebook, and her mind turned to something else. At least for an inning. In the top of the seventh, Tara unexpectedly plopped down in the seat next to me.

"Okay, let's keep score!" Tara said excitedly. I was ready to play along now. I knew this was inevitable.

"All right, but we can't miss anything. I keep track of everything. First pitch results, pitch counts, everything."

"I told you, I've done this before. Hey, what just happened?"

"It was a swinging strike."

"Oh, okay, I'll do good for now on. Hey, do you know Riggans' first name?"

"Yes, it's Shawn."

"Good! That's the same as my fiancé's name. That will make things easier later. Now when I scream out 'Shawn, oh Shawn, oh Shawn,' it won't be cheating!"

"That *is* lucky for you."

"Yeah. I'll talk to him later about tonight. So, am I bothering you?"

"No, not at all. I can hold a conversation and watch a game. It's not hard. I've been doing this a long time. The only problem is sometimes when a pitch count gets high and I have to keep track of the foul balls in my head."

"That's easy. I'm used to having balls in my head."

Geez, I didn't set that one up on a platter for her, did I?

Tara returned to her seat at the end of the half inning, at which point she propositioned Scratch, the Lynx mascot. After some darting come hither looks from Tara, Scratch began his advance towards the veiled vixen. Without any hesitation, she sprung from her seat to kiss him, with tongue, on his fuzzy face. Scratch feigned fainting and fell in my aisle, lying flat on his back a few seats away. Tara hurdled the seat in front of her and began grinding on top of the six-foot furry cat. A family atmosphere, to be sure. Scratch departed to lick his wounds, but returned with a card signed and with his phone number on it. Just as he was leaving, he turned back and sent a wanting look at Tara, thrusting out his bloated middle.

Now, I've seen that bit done by every suited mascot in 200 games, but this seemed just a bit more provocative.

Soccer Moms Unite

How does this continue to happen? Logic and physics say that lightning (and foul balls, in the case of the 50-50 lady in Ottawa) cannot strike in the same place repeatedly. Somehow, Lynx Stadium continues to buck the trend. No way can so many outlandish moments occur in one park in one season.

In just a few visits to Lynx Stadium in Ottawa I've seen a player nearly attack a fan in pre-game, I've seen a managerial meltdown*, I've discovered that a 50-50 lady has a magnetic attraction to foul balls, and I've been accosted by a drunken, soon-to-be bride. This all happened in just a few visits. Throw out opening day and a fairly

---

Dave Trembley's episodic meltdown was easily topped by the Asheville Tourists' manager Joe Mikulik, a sight I witnessed through the miracle of video and the internet. The manager channeled Lou Piniella, Billy Martin and Earl Weaver all at once, sliding into second base, pulling it out to show to the field umpire before tossing it into the outfield, along with his cap. He followed by tossing the rosin bag and made his way to home plate, piling sand on to the dish. After then hurling bats out on to the field from the dugout, he came back with a bottle of water and poured that on home plate to make it muddy. Finally, he left the field and went to the clubhouse, where he apparently ended his tirade by barricading the umpires' locker room with chairs, field screens and anything else he could find. It made Tremblay's argument look like a choirboy taking communion. I just wish I had been there.

non-eventful doubleheader, and my rate of weird occurrences in Ottawa rivals the winning percentage of a Cy Young candidate. However, because of the frequency with which I've already written about Ottawa, I'll try to keep it short.

I arrived late, due to questionable weather patterns on June 30th. Violent thunderstorms were ripping through the northeast so much in late June that sections of the mid-Atlantic region of the United States were flooding. Northern New York and Canada were spared, but that didn't keep the area totally dry. I waited until the last possible moment to leave for Canada and showed up at the ballpark about 45 minutes before game time, which doesn't sound late, but for me anything past the time when the first gates open is tardy. Upon entering the park, I learned that the players had yet to warm up because of the tarp on the field and neither team had taken batting practice, so lengthy preparations by the players would be necessary. Syracuse's starting pitcher, the recently demoted Josh Towers, popped out quickly and made his way to the outfield to do some stretching and jogging to get loose.

Ottawa was filled with promotions that day, just a few hours short of Canada Day, the so-called independence of the dominion from Great Britain attained 140 years earlier. The two winners of *The Amazing Race, Season 9*, BJ and Tyler, were in attendance and caused a huge crowd to show up. Since I don't watch reality television, I had absolutely no clue as to their identities, and I'm proud to say it. Approximately 2,000 others were not so shamed. They stood in line to get autographs that said "BJ" and "Tyler." Outside of random scribbles from busy ballplayers, I eyed a few of these signatures and was embarrassed for the signers. The autographs were in printed block letters with no last names. Twenty years from now, when these photocopied pieces of paper will certainly be valuable Ebay commodities, who will be brought in as experts to examine the validity of the signatures of these two celebrities who enjoyed roughly 15 minutes of fame?

The second promotion did not receive the same fanfare, but should have, considering the action that took place on the field. Five skydivers, from what I can only assume was a portion of the Canadian military, such that it is, were dropped from a few thousand feet and landed in shallow centerfield where a red target was placed beside two small cones set about 20 feet apart. The first three skydivers made flawless landings, making their way through the cones near the target.

Unfortunately for Josh Towers, the fourth wasn't quite so accurate.

Despite the now mostly clear skies, the weather fronts that had recently made their way through Ontario still packed a powerful wind. The fourth skydiver didn't quite gauge the breeze to the best of his abilities and was approximately 120-150 feet off target. It doesn't seem like much, especially in the expanse of grass in the outfield, but the margin made it necessary for some quick movement by Towers. The paratrooper maneuvered his parachute so that he wouldn't crash into the foul pole, batting cage, grandstand or walls, but wasn't quite so careful around the Sky Chiefs' players warming up in the outfield. Towers was nearly dropkicked from the air as the skydiver virtually took the pitcher's hat off on his way down, floating in at what looked like 25-35 miles per hour. Towers was visibly shaken and more divers were on their way. Either the head of promotions or the coordinator of the jumpers was not happy, running out to Towers to berate him. "Silly pitcher, we know this is your job and your preparation is important as you are a former major league player, but could you please get the hell out of the way, we are trying to entertain the 125 people who didn't want the autographs of two guys that no one will recognize after the next season of *Celebrity Fit Club?*" Towers moved to the warning track and mockingly pointed down to ask if he was safe way out there. In Ottawa, you never know.

The game was long and drawn out as Syracuse and Ottawa combined for over 30 hits. In the ninth, trailing by two runs, Ottawa staged a comeback that was both impressive and pathetic. Andy Tracy led off with a double and Luis Terrero followed with a single and a stolen base. Keith Reed walked to load the bases. Pinch-hitter Fernando Tatis (yes, the same Fernando Tatis who hit two grand slams in one inning back in 1999) singled to center to score Tracy, but Terrero held at third to keep the bases loaded, making the score 7-6 with the Lynx trailing. Catcher Eli Whiteside then singled past the shortstop, scoring Terrero to tie the game, but Reed stuck at third when the throw came in quick. An overaggressive Tatis wound up being caught up between second and third and was run down for the first out of the inning. Precisely where Tatis was going, no one in the park was sure. Ottawa was the home team and if Reed scores, the game is over. Of course if Reed is thrown out at home, Tatis should get as close to home as possible, but wouldn't you think his head would be up so he could, you know, *watch the throw*? Oh well, first and third, one out, game tied.

No problem, right?

On the very next pitch, Jason Bowers bunts the ball back to the pitcher, sacrificing the runner over to second. Huh? Did someone miss a sign? Why would you sacrifice a runner over when the winning run is on third already? It surely wasn't a squeeze play because Reed barely budged off third base. Well, fortunately they were now out of the double-play situation, especially since there were now two outs. Whew. Todd Donovan grounded back to the pitcher to end the inning. One of the poorest played innings I've ever seen at the professional level.

There are very few season-ticket holders in Ottawa, but I know many of them pretty well and was seated with them behind home plate. They were not happy and, Mark, one of the younger season-ticket holders, was quite vocal with his displeasure. Not so that the players on the field could hear it, but so that everyone within four rows of our section could hear it. When Syracuse scored three runs on a pair of home runs in the top of the 10th inning, it didn't get better. Mark talked about how the Lynx played terribly the prior inning and they didn't put up much of a fight in their half of the 10th, going down in order.

"Hey, great job, guys," Mark sarcastically remarked. "Way to blow the game."

It was just then that Mrs. Lynx got up and had her turn to express some displeasure.

One of the player's wives or girlfriends, a cute blonde with a nice figure, stood up and started yelling at Mark. It was one of the funniest things I've ever seen, in one of those uncomfortable, squirm-in-your-seat ways.

"You have to watch what you say," she lectured. "You know, you may not be saying things loud to the players, but we can hear you. This is where the players' wives and girlfriends sit. How would you like it if I came down to where you worked and heckled you?"

I giggled out loud at the absurdity. Mark just stood there and took it, but said that she could stop down if she wanted to heckle him.

"I'm going to talk to Kyle about this!" she said ominously, speaking of Kyle Bostwick, the team's general manager.

Mark took it pretty well and I can't wait to find out what the ramifications of her threat entail. She's lucky I wasn't the one who was "heckling" the players and then decided to badger me at the end of the game. I seriously doubt that I could contain my shock at such an unfathomable moment.

Public Speaking 1876: How to Talk to a Baseball Player for Beginners

Three years ago I decided to strike up a conversation with one of the players from the Jamestown Jammers. It was before I knew how to talk to players without sounding like an idiot.

"So how do you like Jamestown," I asked.

"Uck," was the response from Ryan Bear. It was an uncomfortable moment for the two of us; me forcing dialogue and him trying not to get too involved. I sputtered out a response.

"Yeah, I know. I used to live there."

Okay, so I lied. Not only had I never lived in Jamestown, NY, I had never even driven through it. That all changed in early July when my friend Laura invited me to spend a night at her family's lake house just 10 minutes away from the Florida Marlins minor league affiliate.

While I may hate driving through Pennsylvania because of road construction, New York's thruway isn't much better since no one seems capable of getting the hell out of my way. I'm one of those drivers that most people hate because I actually know where I'm going and when I want to get there, so leisurely jaunts on four-lane highways are not what I'm seeking in a five-hour trip. Therefore, Route 90 in New York is not for me because it is a sea of slow drivers and 18-wheelers. After nearly three miserable hours of slowing down below the speed limit every 500 yards, I expected little as I neared the area described by Ryan Bear as "uck."

Magically, as soon as I got off the highway I entered what could only be described as a scene out of the movie *Pleasantville*. The panorama included wide streets, beautiful brick buildings, and houses set back from the road that looked like they were out of a Norman Rockwell painting. I could have sworn I saw two men playing checkers on top of a barrel outside the general store with an American Flag hanging from a pole. I smelled the sweet scent of apple pie.

A few miles down the road was the summer house on Lake Chautauqua. It was a modest dwelling from the outside, but robust on the inside with high ceilings, four levels and numerous modern amenities. I wished that I came earlier than 4 pm, especially since Laura was already half in the bag, having swallowed a couple of toddies awaiting my arrival. Her two golden retrievers greeted me with a couple of barks followed by tail-wagging enthusiasm, and I was off to the backyard to throw sticks into the lake for the two dogs to fetch. In another hour I would be off to a baseball game. Two dogs, a lake house, a baseball team down the road, and a cute, drunk redhead. Could life be any better?

Then I hit Jamestown and I understood Ryan Bear's description. It wasn't that it was an awful place; that would be inaccurate. Jamestown might not be as picturesque as the nearby lake or some of the other small towns that surround it, but it had its own charm. One of the main routes to the ballpark contains uneven brick roads which, to the unaccustomed driver, could be considered quaint or annoying. I chose the former. The park itself, however, was small and was definitely on the lower end of the New York-Penn League's standards. Once again, though, I don't think this is where Ryan Bear had a problem with the town. Bear was born in El Paso, Texas, and then went to school at the University of Central Florida, with 45,000 other undergraduates, under the shadow of Disney in Orlando. Jamestown, compared to most major universities and their neighboring communities, has little population and an even smaller fan base. When a player comes from a large university in the south where teams play in front of several thousand enthusiastic fans with school spirit in their hearts, it is hard to play in undersized stadiums. Jamestown, with a population of around 31,000 people, languishes near the bottom of the NY-Penn's attendance figures with fan totals often reported just over one thousand.

The Jammers' Russell Diethrick Park, opened in 1941, was small and mirrored most of the older NY-Penn parks in the league with standard aluminum bench bleachers down the lines, a small grandstand directly behind the plate and even tinier concession areas. Players walked from the clubhouses next to the concession stands through the concourse to get to the dugouts, which still were not out of the fans reach. I even started to fill out my lineup card on top of the visiting dugout. It was low enough to the ground that it was the perfect height. I would have stayed there the whole game if I wouldn't be blocking anyone's sightline from the bleachers. The view from the first base dugout was nice, too, with the rolling hills of a park behind the left field wall.

Instead I sat with Laura in the grandstand on the third base side, just to the home plate side of the on-deck circle. Laura purchased a beer and was enjoying her drink when the public address announcer alerted everyone that the programs purchased this evening contained special autographs on advertisements inside that were good for prizes. One such prize involved free canine cuisine.

"Ooh, can you check?" Laura asked. "I'm running low on dog food."

This matter-of-fact, but somewhat odd statement drew the attention of a lady sitting immediately in front of us, and she enjoyed a good laugh along with me. Winning dog food isn't usually one of my primary hopes when I buy a ticket for a ballgame. Apparently Laura had higher hopes than nine innings of Short-Season A-ball.

By the fourth inning we were in a full-blown conversation with the lady in front of us. I had already noticed that she seemed particularly interested in one player's success and surmised that she was either a parent or a member of the household that served as a host family for him. Turned out she was mom, the proud parent of Florida's fifth-round pick, Chris Hatcher, a 21-year-old catcher from the University of North Carolina-Wilmington.

Hatcher had started the season slowly, hitting .189 through his first 11 professional games, but he already had his first professional home run and produced 12 runs in 37 at bats. Mom (Kim) and Dad (Dennis) were in Jamestown for the weekend to root for their son, who was a long way from his home in Kinston, NC.

As with most of my friends, Laura has an impressive gift for gab and she chatted away with the lady for the next several innings. We became quite educated about Chris and his collegiate career at UNC-Wilmington. We learned even more about mom. It was, not surprisingly, difficult for Chris's parents to have him so far away in his first taste of professional baseball. After all, his amateur career was played almost exclusively within driving distance of home.

Chris, whose given first name is actually David (a point I felt needed clearing up since I always review the draft lists prior to NY-Penn games and there was some confusion as to what he is normally called), hit .348 with modest power in his junior season at UNC-Wilmington, but sometimes struggled with making contact, whiffing 53 times in 264 at bats. He was the first of six players drafted from the school in 2006 and was selected as the 155th overall pick, signing for a $167,000 bonus. He possesses a strong arm and is a switch-hitter with an athletic frame.

Chris was the epitome of the draft and the NY-Penn League: a mid-level draft pick from a solid Division I school sent to the middle of nowhere to learn how to play the game professionally with its varied equipment (wooden bats) and daily grind. It's also the first place that many draftees get their first true taste of failure. Hitting .189 in 37 at bats is hardly an appropriate sample size to judge a ballplayer, but no one wants to come out of the gate with an average that matches their playing weight. I would have wanted my mom, too.

Having met Chris Hatcher's parents, I'm sure that over the next few years I will periodically check up on his progression through the Florida Marlins' system. He will be around for a while. Clubs don't tend to give up on athletic, switch-hitting catchers clocked at 94 miles per hour off the mound, especially not fifth-round picks that had a couple hundred grand sunk into them for a signing bonus. I didn't stick around to meet Chris, who went 2-for-5 with a pair of triples and two RBI, after the game, since I figured he would be a little more interested in speaking with his parents rather than some guy his parents met in the stands. But I have to think he was a good kid and I will always find myself rooting for him to reach the big leagues. Besides, what do you say to someone you've never met before after talking with their parents for a couple innings?

I found out what not to say in the very same game in which I spoke with Ryan Bear back in 2003. The game was played in Vermont and, thanks to an usher I knew who worked there, I met Josh Whitesell's parents and enjoyed a 10-minute chat with his mother. Whitesell, a sixth-rounder out of Loyola Marymount that year, had just enjoyed a solid game and was signing autographs down the line as he made his way to the clubhouse. Still standing right next to his parents, I reached out and shook his hand and introduced myself as someone who had just spent the last bit of time talking to his parents.

"Your mom speaks very highly of you," I awkwardly said.

As soon as the words left my lips, I thought to myself, what the hell does that mean? Of course his mom speaks highly of him. Even if a son is a convicted felon, a mom will always find the bright side of things. Fortunately, Whitesell recovered from my lunacy, and continued down the line signing autographs for people who thankfully chose not to say anything stupid. I felt like an idiot and concluded that I would never talk to a player about his family ever again. If Chris ever reads this, I'm sure he will thank me in his mind.

Here endeth the lesson.

Ho-tel, Mo-tel, Holiday Inn Becomes Leggo My Ego

Any kind of all-star game fanfest festivities reminds me of a 20-second bit used on *The Simpsons*. Homer goes off into a sort of haze at the thought of "the land of chocolate" and he is seen skipping and prancing with grinning bunnies through a magical wonderland of chocolate. Homer bites lampposts (made of chocolate) and barking dogs (made of chocolate) before coming to a window where he ogles a sign that reads "chocolate, half-price."

Fanfests have so much activity going on, fans don't know where to start and suddenly they see memorabilia dealers pushing baseball cards, posters, and autographed pictures for ridiculous sums. However, the fans are so dizzy from all of the other activities surrounding them, they figure what's 65 bucks for an autographed 8x10 photo of former Pirates reliever Cecillio Guante. Fortunately, I've been to enough of these to know that you can't let your emotions get the best of you. It's okay to take a look around and see a bunch of cool stuff, but you must stay focused on your itinerary. My agenda for the MLB All-Star Fanfest in Pittsburgh was the meet-and-greet with the participants in the Futures Game at 11 a.m. that morning. It would be at most an hour, so there would be plenty of time to look at other things.

I arrived around 9:30 a.m. and was immediately given a bag full of goodies, including the new *Baseball America* periodical with information about the Futures Game participants. I reviewed the magazine and took a look around at the lower level of the convention center. A line that stretched for several hundred yards was to my left, which I knew had to be the line for free autographs from the local legends and Hall of Famers signed up for the event. The amazing thing here was that there were no former players on the stage. I shook my head in disbelief, knowing there was no way I would want to waste my time on that, especially since there was no definitive schedule posted for any particular player. These people could end up standing in line for Mudcat Grant and Doc Ellis for all they knew. But there are some people who live and die for signatures of former ballplayers. I like autographs of my favorites as much as the next person, but not in order to sacrifice my day, or days in the case of this weekend event.

Nope, I was focused. My agenda was upstairs for the meet-and-greet with the future stars of baseball. Unless I got sidetracked.

It was 10 a.m. and there was plenty of time to take a look around upstairs before the minor leaguers would be announced on the miniature ball field in the center of the David L. Lawrence Convention Center. There was nothing occurring on the field at that time, just a few people setting things up for the next clinic, when I heard my own personal siren call.

"Where was the 1938 All-Star game played?" came from the distance.

"Crosley Field," I said to myself. The only reason I knew that was because it was the same year that Cincinnati Reds pitcher Johnny Vander Meer pitched his consecutive no-hitters, and he pitched in that All-Star game. Nonetheless, the sweet sound of baseball trivia was emanating from yonder and I was sure to seek it out.

A few dozen benches were set up inside an area that could fit approximately 200 people. Three participants sat on the stage of the "Fanfest Challenge" with an attractive woman spitting rapid-fire questions at them. Buzzers were in place and one guy was cleaning up the competition, such that it was. Average questions were tossed at the participants and I cruised through the last few rounds without any problems, shaking my head after every missed question. The ladies in the back smiled at me as I murmured answers to questions before the multiple choice answers even arrived on the screen.

"I've got to get up there. How do you get on stage?" I asked one of them.

"Oh, just sit up front and you will get picked," answered a lady in a Fanfest smock.

As soon as the last question was asked and answered, the stage was cleared. It would be another 10 minutes before the next contest, but I thought there would be plenty of time before the Futures Game participants would be introduced directly behind me.

I sat in the front row, lying in wait to get up on stage to blow away these huckleberries with my baseball knowledge. I love trivia challenges in just about anything thanks to a useless pile of information that accumulates in my mind, but baseball trivia is another world for me. Back in 1994, I was at a friend's New Year's Eve party and around 8:30 we were talking about decade old music and it somehow brought out a baseball question: Who won the World Series MVP in 1985?

"Darrell Porter," said Dan, up until then only an acquaintance of mine.

"No, it was Bret Saberhagen," I said.

"Kansas City won in 1985, right?" Dan came back.

"Yeah, and Saberhagen won the MVP of that World Series. Darrell Porter won with the Cardinals in 1982," I explained. "Darrell Porter played with Kansas City at one point, but it wasn't in 1985."

We went back and forth until a sports almanac found its way over from the bookshelf. Naturally, I was right; but a friendship was born as Dan and I went back and forth with baseball trivia for the next four hours, much to the chagrin of our girlfriends. For the next few years, Dan and I would convene at the library to play chess and volley baseball questions and answers. To some the meetings may sound like a kind of nerd-fest, but for us it was a way of serenely keeping our minds sharp, with all of life's other distractions. Besides, our girlfriends quickly tired of the routine that had started the previous

New Year's Eve. Eventually, Dan ran out of things to ask or started to repeat himself, but it didn't matter. Just finding someone who enjoyed the game and its history in a similar fashion was enough.

Surrounded by a bunch of people who Dan would have throttled with his baseball trivia made me nervous. What if I lost? What if some other guy who devoured baseball information was sitting behind me? What if Raymond Babbitt from *Rain Man* was in the back corner rocking back and forth, ready to spring the career batting average of Gus Zernial upon the unsuspecting crowd?

The master of ceremonies came out with a headset and started talking about the trivia challenge's sponsor, Holiday Inn Hotels. She was energetic and fun, the perfect emcee. It was at that point she scared the hell out of me.

"Before we get started, first I'm going to pick our contestants by asking questions about our sponsor, Holiday Inn."

"Oh, shit," I said under my breath.

"First, what hotel chain officially sponsors major league baseball?"

I didn't bother to even raise my hand as dozens shot up all around me. It was like being a paleontologist in a kindergarten class and having someone ask the group a dinosaur question that revolved around Barney. It just wasn't fair that this was how selections would be made for a baseball trivia contest. A 10-year-old named Brandon correctly came up with "Holiday Inn."

"Okay, next question. How many Holiday Inns are there in the United States? One thousand, 10 thousand or 1 million?"

I didn't even bother as a few dozen hands went up again. Someone said the wrong answer and then an 18-year-old was called on and picked the right one in what was now a fifty-fifty shot. I don't even know what ended up being the correct answer because my eyes were rolling to the back of my head. My heart was sinking, and everything I held near and dear about baseball trivia was being questioned. It was great that Holiday Inn was philanthropic enough to sponsor the booth and all, but this wasn't right. I was panicking and my world was falling apart around me.

"Okay, last question. What 80s rap group..."

Thank God. My hand shot up.

"...sang the lyrics, 'hotel, motel, Holiday Inn' in their famous song?"

My hand fluttered about in the air, praying it was the first one up. I felt like an overzealous, know-it-all third-grader.

"Wow, I didn't even have to finish the question," the emcee said. "Yes, you?"

"The Sugarhill Gang," I answered triumphantly. If anyone's life ever hung in the balance and would live or die with me answering a question about baseball, they would probably be safe. The same could be said for trivia about music from the 80s and 90s. I know the order in which songs were released from albums in 1988, I know what the peak chart position was for "Don't You (Forget About Me)" by Simple Minds from 1985, and I sure as hell know the lyrics to the song "Rapper's Delight" by the Sugarhill Gang, which incidentally was released late in 1979, not in the 80s, but I wasn't going to argue.

I hopped on to the stage and saw my competition: a 10-year-old and a guy who probably impresses his boys during the post-season by telling them the Yankees have won the most World Series titles. I decided to start slow to build the drama and not look like a total ass. Without pushing my buzzer, I fell behind by 100 points pretty quickly. The emcee looked nervous, like she had allowed a dead fish on her stage.

"You doing okay down there, Tommy?" she asked, the concern blatantly worn on her pretty face.

"Yup," I responded, expecting the question. "I'll get going soon."

It didn't help that these questions were multiple choice and really simple. It was the opening round and categories like "history" and "stats" were still lingering unmarked on the board. Both players were now over 100 points ahead of me, so I decided to join the fray. I answered four straight questions to jump back into contention and took off from there. By the end of the round, I took the lead with 360 points, but was ahead of the 18-year-old by only 50 points, thanks to his answering a couple of "double jeopardy" questions. The emcee asked the crowd who they felt the eventual winner would be. Besides the relatives of the other participants, the crowd voted for me in a landslide, even if they weren't rooting for me. I didn't blame them. I wouldn't have encouraging thoughts for me, either, since I was beating up on a couple of kids.

My ego would not let me lose, though. There would be no passive actions in the second round as I stepped up my play, receiving both of the extra-point chances and jumping out to a several-hundred point advantage. With a score now swelling well over 1,000 going into the final round and just one final question left up for grabs, I couldn't decide how to wager my collection of points. Should I risk it all and try to get as many points as possible for my ego's sake, or just wager enough to ensure a victory? I chose the latter, but the final question made me wish I had gone for ego.

"Who is the only player in major league history to steal more than 100 bases in his first three seasons?" the emcee said, reading from her screen.

As a kid, with a brain like a sponge for statistics, growing up in the 1980s, I didn't need options. Vince Coleman of the St. Louis Cardinals was the only rookie to ever reach 100 steals, swiping 110 bags in 1985. He broke Juan Samuel's year-old mark of 72 steals in 1984, which broke the three-year old record by Tim Raines when he swiped 71 bases in the strike-shortened season of 1981 (interestingly, the strike robbed Raines of the opportunity to steal 100 in one year since the teams only completed two-thirds of the schedule). Coleman also came up with 107 steals in 1986 and 109 in 1987. I could have quoted all of this right then and there, but instead maintained my poker face. My posture must have been a giveaway to the crowd, though, because when I looked out at the people, most were looking directly at me, supposing that this contest was over and done. I'm not trying to brag here, the question wasn't hard and neither was the contest. I've never lost a baseball trivia challenge with anyone and I sure wasn't about to start in a multiple-choice contest against a pair of contestants I could have beaten while heavily sedated. That said, if the 200 or so people in attendance weren't cheering me before, they would at least like me in the end.

After revealing that my answer was correct to all of those in attendance, the emcee was ready to let me jump into a plastic box resembling a phone booth with prizes blowing around me, but I couldn't let that happen. I called her over and told her to let 10-year-old Brandon have my prize. After all, I was here for the Futures Game, not to look like an idiot flailing about in a plastic booth.

Brandon's face brightened up like the passing sun outside when the emcee repeated my charity for the day, and the moment I stepped off the stage to applause, his father ran over to me and shook my hand heartily, thanking me as if I had just pulled his son out of a burning building.

"No problem," I said as I slung my backpack over my shoulder and picked my way through the crowd to the exit. It reminded me of a 1950s western with the protagonist riding his horse out of the town he had just saved, eliminating all of those despicable outlaws. Yup, the lonesome cowboy known simply as "Tommy" had won and was the hero of the day, I reckon.

My ego knows no bounds.

Tribute Night

Any time someone asks me what my favorite park in minor league baseball is, I frequently blow them away with the answer: Centennial Field in Burlington, Vermont.

I can't blame it on the fact that I've been there so many times because I loved it the first time I went. Amazingly, this year it was given an honorable mention nod at the end of the list of top 10 parks in the minors, so apparently I'm not alone. I have come to know a few people that work at the park, most specifically one of the ushers named Hillary, with whom I've become friends over the past few seasons. She has given me so much inside information on the players and the park that I feel as if I've worked there. A few seasons ago she pointed out Salomon Manriquez's wife, who always sat in the same spot and kept score of the games or, at the very least, her husband's at bats. She introduced me to Josh Whitesell's parents, something I wish she had never done because of the aforementioned idiotic comment I made to him. She also let me know that a gawky 18-year-old was dating one of the young Dominican players and that the girl was hoping to ride the wave all the way to the major leagues. My adoration for Centennial Field is not all about familiarity with people in the stands or small-town rumors and gossip, for the latter is something I can do without. There is one significant, overall attribute that makes me love this stadium.

Centennial Field is a dump. And I mean that in the nicest possible way.

ABNER'S CURSE:
A DIARY OF ESSAYS FROM A BASEBALL ITENERANT

The first game ever played at Centennial Field was a college contest in 1906 and the current grandstand was constructed in 1922, when frills were far from a necessity at a stadium. There are great iron beams in the middle of the reserved sections, blocking some views. The roofs of the dugouts look like particleboard with one fine layer of lacquered sheetrock on top to assure a smooth finish for the painting of advertisements. The reserved seats are wooden and uncomfortable enough to require the inhabitants a third inning, fifth inning and seventh inning stretch. Those wooden seats are like a Lazy-Boy recliner compared to the concrete steps that make up the general admission section on both sides of the reserved section behind home plate. In fact, after the first inning, one of the promotions is for a general admission ticket holder and friend to take up residency in a pair of upholstered easy chairs, seemingly taken right out of your neighbor's living room, set up on the third base line of the concrete slabs.

The home clubhouse on the first base side is situated close by so that the players can just saunter out of the locker room once they have prepared themselves for the game. The area isn't really fenced off, and on this particular day, when I walked up the ramp on the first base side along the concourse, I could look right in and see a couple players messing around with one another as they strolled down the hallway.

But that is luxury compared to the visitors' accommodations. Beyond the left field wall at Centennial Field is a soccer field and its grandstand, where the University of Vermont Catamounts' booters play (the Catamounts use the baseball field before the Lake Monsters take over from mid-June to early-September). Well beyond the soccer field is where the visitors change, in what I can assume is the soccer locker room. It's a short 150-yard walk for the visitors to get to their dugout, the last 60 yards going right through the picnic and concession area to get through a four-foot gate to the bullpen on the third base line.

While the park's seating area and amenities are monstrosities compared to the newer ballparks in the league, the field is oozing with charm and an old-time feel. The warning track all around the park used to serve as a running track, creating so much foul ground that the Oakland Coliseum is jealous. Remember the Derek Jeter catch in 2004 when Jeter ran a few extra steps after making his overrated catch in fair territory and dove headlong into the stands (for no explicable reason, I might add—I watched the play again recently on video and still don't understand why he dove) against the Red Sox during the 2004 season? Second baseman Michael Martinez attempted to make a catch down the right field line midway through the game that would have had him in the 10th row of the box seats at Yankee Stadium. And he still had another 30 feet before someone would warn him about the fence.

Ever since my first visit to the ballpark in July 2003, I was baffled at the amount of foul territory, especially behind home plate. One could imagine a fastball rolling to a stop before reaching the end of that much real estate, almost like a bullet in an open field finally losing the battle versus friction and dropping to the earth. I asked Hillary the first time I went to the park how much space there was between home plate and backstop. She didn't know. It looked to be considerably more than the distance from home plate to the pitcher's mound. I asked if she could find out, but she never could give me an answer. I even requested an opportunity to go down on the field with a tape measure to figure it out.

For some reason that fall, after the close of the 2003 season, I noticed a note on the Vermont website from general manager CJ Knudsen thanking all of those who attended games during the season. He had his email on the note for anyone who wanted to make a comment. I replied to his open email about how much I enjoyed his park and the atmosphere despite the team's awful record of 19-57. I recall mentioning to him that the team completed a perfect 5-0 record when I was in attendance. He responded that if the team could go 10-0 with me in the stands the following season that he would give me season tickets.

Although July 15th was my third visit to Centennial Field in the 2006 season, it was the first time that anything remarkable occurred.

Sure, the previous games had been entertaining (a quick 1-0 game against Tri-City and a tough 3-2 loss to Lowell ten days later), but it wasn't like I had been accosted by a drunken bachelorette. That's one of many reasons I love Centennial Field. It's a crisp atmosphere where the promotions are important and fans can still have excellent interactions with the players, but the game is primary on the agenda. I've never heard a negative comment from anyone in attendance about the opposing team or the home team. No heckling, just cheering (especially late in the game when the public address announcer gives the scores from the major league games, with extra emphasis on anything involving the Red Sox or Yankees).

It's these kinds of conditions in which games should always be played. Part of it is because so many of these players have recently been drafted and they are thrilled to be playing ball professionally. Most of them won't ever make it out of A-ball. Though they all hope to make it to the major leagues, deep down the players know there is a better chance they'll be selling insurance or working in an office building inside of a year. Full-season ball offers only 100 jobs per major league team in the minor leagues and every year over 1,500 players get drafted, which still does not include international players. If all of those 1,500 players were to make it in full-season ball the next season, that would be half of the jobs in the minors. Obviously, some of the boys are going home after *this* season. And they won't be coming back. Needless to say, it makes for a lot of modesty among the players, understanding the long odds of making it to the big leagues. It also makes for a great deal of tenacity in the action on the field. If someone is lollygagging their way around the base paths or in the outfield, they are likely not long for that game or the league.

The first item on my checklist for this specific game was to meet CJ Knudsen, the general manager. We had sent a few emails back and forth over the previous weeks as I was trying to get some minor league franchises to send items for door prizes for a golf outing that I was helping to organize. It didn't take long for me to find him. He was cordial, a very nice guy, and most importantly, he answered a question for which I had longed an answer for over three years: 90

feet from home plate to back stop. It was as if a heavy burden was finally removed from my mind.

It was "A Tribute to Montreal" night in Vermont, the second annual such night. In 2005, I was geared up to attend the tribute night because the honorary guest was Andre Dawson and I was rather excited about the opportunity to meet the Hawk. Unfortunately, it rained (not Shea Stadium rain, but thunderstorms) and I didn't want to waste the time and money to go to Centennial Field for the game when it was just going to get washed out. It's a 280-mile round trip with no major highways and I wasn't too interested in driving to Burlington and back. But son of a bitch, they got the game in and I missed it.

The 2006 version of tribute night wasn't quite Andre Dawson in my estimation, but I was still pretty excited to meet Dennis Martinez, nicknamed "El Presidente" by his countrymen of Nicaragua. Rain was in the forecast again, but I was not to be denied on this night. I went anyway and for my trip I was greeted not only by Dennis Martinez, but also by a cast of characters that was unparalleled in any trip I've ever made. It wasn't so much the nuttiness of the characters' actions or what any of them said. In fact, I never spoke with any of them. It just would have felt odd talking to so many celebrities. Or, at least, celebrity look-a-likes.

I attended the game with my friends Scott, Erika and Hillary (who has moved on from ushering to bigger and better things) among other later arrivals, but I was unable to pay much attention to my friends because of the oddballs surrounding me. First, we had spent no more than five minutes in the rain-soaked stadium when Scott told me that Don Zimmer was behind us. I turned around and, yup, there was an old guy who looked just like Don Zimmer, former major league manager and oddball himself who will likely best be remembered for rolling around on the ground after he bull-rushed Pedro Martinez in a bench-clearing episode in 2003 at Fenway Park. While the Zimmer twin was an intriguing addition to the ballpark, it was Hall of Fame reliever Dennis Eckersley who gained most of my attention. He was sitting just a few seats down from Zimmer. The Eck looked a little shorter than usual, but the hair was unmistakable. It had to be him! Either Eckersley or maybe Yanni. Being a baseball fan, I had Eck in my head as opposed to a Greek composer. When I went to my seats an hour later, Eck was still walking around shaking hands with people (it had to be him!), when I suddenly saw Lou Piniella walk through one of the corridors coming from the concourse. It had to be him! He was wearing a Vermont Lake Monsters pullover, just like Lou used to wear when he was coaching for the Devil Rays. But why would Lou be here? He had no connection with the Lake Monsters (clearly Zim and Eck did, right?), and he seemed more interested in making sure no one took his seat. Lastly, though not a baseball player, a combination of deceased funny man Chris Farley and former professional wrestler Bryan Knox (from the 1990s tag team known as the Nasty Boys) was sitting right in front of me! The hair was indescribable. Words cannot do it justice, so I won't try. Blonde mullets everywhere are proud. Parades are formed and statues are erected.

Walking around the stadium on several trips (remember, the seats aren't so comfortable) I noticed several things about these men. Their commitment to character was consistent. Zim was stoic in his seat. The Nasty Boy/Farley conglomeration enjoyed food. Eck was a crowd pleaser and a social butterfly. Piniella, well, he contained himself from yelling at the umpires.

With so many celebrities around, it was difficult to get excited about Dennis Martinez. My enthusiasm waned, but I still needed to get his autograph on a couple of old baseball cards from my unforgotten youth, so in the second inning I got in line to grab a couple of signatures from the 245-game winner. One guy in front of me decided to strike up a conversation with El Presidente, which normally would have irritated me since I was trying to get Martinez's signature in the middle of the inning without missing any of the game, but it wasn't a long line. The two discussed the 1981 strike season in which Martinez started off very well and looked to possibly be on his way to a Cy Young award, having won a league-best 14 games (tied with several other pitchers). Martinez did correctly recall that Rollie Fingers won the Cy Young Award, but he told the guy it was the first time they had ever given the award to a reliever. Or maybe he meant it was the first time they had ever given the MVP award to a relief pitcher. No matter, as he was wrong both times. Bruce Sutter won the Cy Young in the National League in 1979 and Sparky Lyle won the Cy Young award in the American League just a few years earlier, while Jim Konstanty won the MVP award for the Philadelphia Phillies back in 1950.

I can't blame Martinez for having his facts wrong. With all the celebrities in the house, I would have been flustered, too. Wait a minute...was that really Dennis Martinez?

Coming This July—Cooperstown: Abner's Curse

For nearly 70 years, the National Baseball Hall of Fame has inducted new members in to its hallowed halls. As most people know, the first election was in 1936 with a five-player class including Ty Cobb, Babe Ruth, Honus Wagner, Walter Johnson and Christy Mathewson, but the actual museum did not open until three years later. Since the museum's opening, over 200 players, managers, executives, and contributors have been enshrined in Cooperstown, NY, many of which enjoyed memorable ceremonies on glorious summer days.

My first trip to Cooperstown came in 1985 when I was still young and impressionable. My little legs took me all over the museum, and my family spent the entire day inside, save for a couple of swings and throws at the Doubleday batting range. Back then, my sponge-like mind gathered all pieces of information that it could and took them as fact. Most pre-teen children are like that: kids are willing to accept just about any theory and regard it as the truth. It isn't until the teenage years that we begin to question ideals. It's probably a combination of maturation of the mind and rebellion against whatever authority is in front of us.

And this is where the curse of Abner Doubleday begins.

Abner Doubleday was handed the title of "Inventor of Baseball" almost 100 years ago because of pride and necessity. Members of the baseball hierarchy desperately wanted to believe that the game of baseball was purely an American enterprise and was begun with their ingenuity, especially since Europeans mocked the game as an amalgamation of cricket and rounders (as if Europeans didn't already mock everything else in American society at that time; we certainly couldn't have them attacking *our* game). A national search, such that it was, came across information that Abner Doubleday invented the game in Cooperstown, NY, in 1839. If this were the movie *Braveheart,* he also would have been 10-feet tall and lightning bolts would have come out of his arse.

Doubleday did exist, but he had nothing to do with the invention of baseball. It's a lovely myth, especially since Doubleday was a Civil War hero, but it is much more likely that Alexander Cartwright put the first legitimate rules of the game forth in 1846 when a pair of teams played on the Elysian Fields in Hoboken, New Jersey. In the past few years, further "fossil records" regarding baseball's birth came in the way of the discovery of a law that was passed in Pittsfield, Massachusetts, during the 18th century, disallowing the game of "base" from being played within certain distances of local businesses. The breaking of windows by baseballs is clearly a centuries old problem.

All of the Abner Doubleday disinformation came to me in my teenage years and, much like the rumors of Santa Claus coming down the chimney to give children a bounty of gifts (only my house didn't have a traditional chimney, making the trip unquestionably snug as Santa slunk his way through the pipes of our heating system), the truth I knew as a child melted away. It would be eight years before I could return to Cooperstown and by that time I had so angered the spirit of Abner Doubleday, he would curse my knowledge and bring about pestilence and misery in baseball's Mecca every time I visited hereafter.

In 1993, my father's back was bothering him so much on the car ride down to Cooperstown that we spent almost as much time on the grass in a local park as we did inside the museum. Two years later, a group of friends came along with me and we did have a great time, but I blew out my arm at Doubleday Field with the pitching challenge as the four of us combined to drop about $120 over the course of two hours trying to see if we could hit 70 miles per hour on the radar gun (four years of non-throwing activity for the four of us pretty much slammed the door shut on any possibility of the elusive 70 reading). My arm was so sore that I would wait for it to go numb before I would get up and throw again.

The winter before my final semester of college I was working on my senior thesis regarding Curt Flood and the advent of free agency in baseball and needed to utilize the Hall of Fame library's vast collection. The trip was so depressing that I refused to go back to Cooperstown for years. When I walked into the Hall of Fame those cold January days, I was the only person in the museum. There are already ghosts in Cooperstown; you can feel the past rush through your body every time you step into the museum. It's a different feeling than other museums because this history is recent and some of those enshrined as baseball immortals are still walking the streets each July. Well, my echoing footsteps in the room full of plaques created uneasiness in my soul. It was as if this was a time of rest for baseball's greats. The summer was when the pageantry of Cooperstown and its museum came through, and the players were always up to task. But now was their time for slumber and here I was tramping my way through the gallery as an intruder.

Though that winter trip opened my eyes to the specters of Cooperstown, I did finally return in 2003 with Ryan and Dave as the last stop on an eight-day trip of ballparks in the mid-Atlantic region. Neither of my friends had a fraction of my knowledge, nor had they ever been to Cooperstown, so both wandered through the museum taking in everything. This turned out to be a godsend since it was pouring rain outside, a theme that would follow me for the next few years in my trips to the induction ceremonies. Abner's curse was alive and well.

I hate to sound melodramatic, but it seems as if Abner's curse has grown in power this year, stretching out its evil hand well beyond the mysterious borders of Cooperstown. A large cloud of rain-filled misery has followed me in 2006. Poor weather at the beginning of the minor league season kept me from seeing Delmon Young's meltdown in Pawtucket in late-April while a fast-moving low pressure system ended my first trip to Cooperstown in May when I hoped to attend the annual Hall of Fame game between the Cincinnati Reds and Pittsburgh Pirates. Flooded streets in New York City finished off all hope of seeing Barry Bonds against the New York Mets in early June, and a five-hour misty rain delay at Fenway Park tried my patience. A mere eight days later a downpour in Cleveland shortened my stay at Jacobs Field. However, these wretched and gloomy days were a walk in the park compared to Cooperstown's Induction Weekend 2006.

My first-ever trip for Induction Weekend came in 2004, but I only stayed for the first two days because I was so miserable. Without going into much detail, it was 80 degrees with 95 percent humidity at night and I was sleeping in the back of my jeep at my friend Tony's rented campsite. The sleeping constituted about an hour of restlessness before I decided to get out and sleep on the ground, unprotected from the elements. It rained lightly and a skunk waddled by about 10 feet away before I returned to the safety of my jeep. All told, I might have slept for 45 minutes before showering. It then rained all day on Friday, wiping out any outdoor festivities. The downpour was so considerable I actually soaked my spark plugs going through a puddle near the Otesaga Hotel where all of the returning Hall of Fame members stayed for the weekend. Security wouldn't allow me to use the phone (I was incredibly irritated at the time, but in retrospect I'm sure the guards were just doing their jobs), so I had to walk all the way into town where I was kept on hold for 30 minutes, in the rain, on an outdoor pay phone, only to be told that my warranty had run out and I would be dropping more than $100 for a tow truck. Fortunately, my spark plugs dried and I canceled the tow truck, along with the rest of my trip. I returned to the campsite and bailed, cutting my losses. I did meet Kirby Puckett and Jim Palmer on the golf course and obtained both players' signatures on their respective autobiographies that I had brought along with me.*

Though I once again spent a couple of restless evenings in my new car in 2005, the nights were at least devoid of unbearable heat and the pitter-patter of rain. It was a much better time (though I somehow repeatedly injured my ankle in both the batting cages and any time I tried to move my right foot forward), and I journeyed out of Cooperstown on a few nights to see minor league games in both Binghamton and Oneonta. The trip was enjoyable and without any major negatives, other than a long night spent in nearby Clinton, NY, with a friend of mine who decided that we both needed to stay up until four in the morning. Since I stayed up that long the year before, tossing and turning with a seatbelt stabbing my vertebrae, it was a welcome change.

My trips to Cooperstown for Induction Weekend constitute a few diversions. First and foremost, is going to the golf course to try to get free autographs from the Hall of Famers during their tournament. It's not easy, and if you can get one per day with all of the pushing and shoving that goes on, you are doing well. From 7 a.m. to noon, Tony, his son, and I cheer on the baseball golfers in hopes that they will grant the hundreds of autograph seekers two minutes of their time. After the golfing is over, generally we go into town and walk around. I've been in the Hall of Fame so many times at this point that I usually

---

* *An amusing aside: In 2004, along with Tony and his son Matt, I was with the son of an acquaintance, also named Matt. The second Matt was eagerly trying to get Kirby Puckett's autograph and did not know who the other golfer was with Kirby. In all honesty, because he was wearing a panama hat and sunglasses, I didn't immediately recognize his partner either. The partner reached out his hand to sign the baseball, but Matt pulled it away. Tony, a seasoned veteran at the golf course, then jumped in and said, "Jim!" Palmer quickly answered, "Nope." We did get Kirby on the 9th hole, but could not obtain Mr. Palmer's autograph until the 12th hole when he had calmed down after being dissed by a 17-year-old on Hall of Fame weekend who thought he was simply a member of the country club. Apparently the ego can still be bruised even after 20 years of retirement.*

don't go inside. Instead, I just mill about town, grab some pizza, window shop in the stores with exorbitantly priced items (five dollars for a Shannon Stewart?), and spend time at Doubleday Field. When the time in town is completed, we return to the campsite to regale in our triumphs or talk baseball. Then we head to the batting cages to rip open our palms by swinging undersized aluminum bats at rubber baseballs. A quick jaunt back up to the golf course to make sure there are no stragglers is the next order of business, and then it's back downtown or to the campsite for the night. If the schedule cooperates, I'll fit in a minor league game or two at Oneonta or Binghamton.

The positive memories from 2005 made July 27-30 appear to be the highlight of this year. There are two things that I look forward to each baseball season more than anything else: Minor League All-Star games and Cooperstown. I attended both the South Atlantic League All-Star Game in Eastlake, Ohio, and the Futures Game in Pittsburgh and enjoyed both tremendously. I anticipated as much in my weekend in Central New York.

Little did I know that Abner's curse was surging to the level of an endemic plague.

About a week or two before the Cooperstown pilgrimage, I decided to brighten up a bit and I purchased a tent. Two years of sleeping in vehicles had left me weary and wary. Unfortunately, as wise as I might have been for buying the tent, my wisdom ended there. I arrived at the campsite about an hour past noon on Thursday with Tony and his other compatriots setting up. I didn't really want to get in the way of their construction of the camper, so I cleaned up my car and prepared for the next few hours at the golf course. That preparation did not include me setting up my tent. We would have plenty of time for that later, or so I thought. Following the golf course, where Phil Niekro stopped to sign, and a trip downtown, we came back to the campsite around 7 p.m. and I immediately went to the makeshift basketball court to shoot around for a few minutes. Those few minutes turned into two hours, and by the time I walked back to the site, I had no desire to put the tent up. It was dark amidst the light-blocking trees and I really just wanted to sit down. When 11 p.m. rolled around, I decided to just sleep in my car again, feeling way too lazy to put up the tent this late. Seventy-five minutes of recalling how uncomfortable it was to sleep in a humid car, along with noisy neighbors keeping me up, I pulled my car out of the campsite and moved it to the more secluded overflow campground across the street where one of Tony's friends was staying. I backed in to the most remote corner of the grassy area, roughly the size of two or three football fields and rolled down the windows. The night was peaceful, not too hot with the windows down. Of course, when you are parked next to a swamp with trees and tall grass you quickly recall that nature is against you. Mosquitoes spent the next hour dive-bombing my ears and head, making for more discomfort. Now near 1:30 in the morning with no sign of sleep in sight, I decided to pull up stakes and drive to the golf course. I figured if I was going to be awake all night, I might as well make use of it.

What possible sense would it make to go to the golf course six hours before any sensible golfer would tee off, one might wonder. Well, there is a fat sports card dealer from New York City or New Jersey who always gets the best spot at the golf course, right at the ninth hole. Nearly every baseball golfer stops to sign autographs there, right by the tees, and every year that fat dealer seems to get there first. And this early Friday morning, I discovered why. He sleeps there. I drove past the golf course at 1:45 and there were three people taking up nearly 25 feet of space, sleeping on fold out chairs. I couldn't help but laugh. Part of me wanted to stop by and honk my horn for about 20 minutes, but I held off.

After circling the golf course, I continued to drive around in search of lodging, desperate for sleep. I had spent the past three days in Connecticut, watching five minor league games in New Britain and Norwich, but sleep could not be found there for some inexplicable reason. I slept, on average, for three or four hours per night in Connecticut, and the deprivation exhausted me. Fortunately, Bruce Sutter was the only living member of the 2006 Induction

Class, and for the first time in years there was actually vacancy at some of the local hotels. For thirty minutes I made my way into parking lots in hopes of finding space. Finally, a Howard Johnson's seemed the best place to go (alas, Holiday Inn's advertisements at the Fanfest Challenge were lost on me). A surprisingly fresh face in the HoJo met mine, which was certainly downtrodden and haggard at 2:10 in the morning.

"Hi," I greeted the lady behind the counter. "I have two questions. First, do you have any vacancy in the hotel? Second, how much is it going to cost?"

"Well, we do have some vacancy," she responded with delight as her fingernails danced upon the keyboard in front of her. I'm guessing she was on pep pills. "All we have are King Suites left and they are $240 a night."

I looked at her blankly. It was 2:10 in the morning. There was no way this room was going to be filled. I was looking for five hours of sleep and a shower, not a massage with a happy ending.

"Two hundred and forty?" I said. "All I want to do is get a few hours of sleep."

"That's our rate," she smiled back.

"I'd rather stay up all night," I said without returning a toothy grin and trudged my way back through the automatic doors, which proved more useful than usual since I lacked the strength to push them open. A friend of mine had, on many occasions, told me how he had stopped at hotels late at night and was able to get cut rates because an empty room at that point served no purpose to the hotel. Made sense to me, but I guess it was lost on cheery, middle-aged hotel lobby workers in Cooperstown.

I drove to a town about 12 miles from Cooperstown that actually had streetlights, and hopped out of my car to look into the trunk at my unassembled tent. I cursed my laziness as my hands fumbled about in the dark trunk. Not only were the directions for the tent hard to understand after several days of insomnia, but also the numerous poles and flapping plastic proved to be more difficult to solve than a Rubik's Cube. Slamming the trunk and cursing more, I drove on to a rest stop just a few miles shy of Oneonta. The rest stop was something out of a horror movie. A pair of abandoned flat beds populated the broken tar as weed saplings made their way through the faults in the concrete. It took me little time to decide this was more likely to be my final resting place than a place for a three-hour nap.

Driving back toward Cooperstown, the clock crept towards 3:00 a.m. and I was getting desperate. Back in the town where I had parked earlier to check the tent directions, a large building loomed in the distance. I drove around its massive parking lot and found that it was a hospital. Parking near a storage shed at the very end of the lot underneath a giant light, I figured this barren lot of blacktop was good enough. With such a light glaring above me, I assumed all the bugs would stay away from the heat of my body and I could finally sleep. Two hours and twenty minutes of restless sleep passed and the dawn was starting to break. It was time to hustle back to the campground for a shower.

I'd like to brag that the whole ordeal was worth it, but Abner Doubleday's apparition was showing no mercy. Friday was miserable. It sprinkled off and on for much of the day and my time at the golf course proved to be a literal wash as the sprinkling turned into a heavy downpour that prompted me to consider purchasing a canoe. Twelve hours after finally falling asleep the night before, I thought of the tent. Tony said that had I put the tent up it would have kept all the rain out and while that was true, he said nothing of the possibility that the tent could have floated away as the campsite became more sludge than bedded forest. The prospect of another night of sleeping in my car in the parking lot of some vacant hospital was not sitting well. At 3:30 Friday afternoon, I decided to call it a day and drove to a far off bed.

The following morning I rolled out of bed around 4:30 a.m. and drove back to Cooperstown for what was supposed to be a beautiful Saturday, but the strength of Abner's curse continued to grow like a scourge with every passing hour. A new low was about to be achieved in Cooperstown.

On Saturday afternoon my group went to the batting cages to take our annual hacks at the best pitching machines in the area. Close to an hour after arriving, the cloudiness turned into a dark gray cloud of pure menace. While departing the fun park we were told that a tornado touched down just 40 miles away and the storm was making its way toward Cooperstown. I laughed out loud and was not intimidated by Mother Nature. She had already slapped me around enough this year. There was no way a tornado would sweep me into the air and put me out of my misery.

No, there was no way that a tornado would hit. However, the rain that came 20 minutes later made Friday feel like spittle. In the time that it took Tony, his son, Matt, and me to get from a Stewart's Shop to the campsite, a distance of about two miles, at least an inch of rain dropped from the sky. The wind picked up with heavy gusts that knocked tree limbs into the already narrow roadway and less than half a mile to the campsite, Tony's SUV was met with a challenge in the road: Abner had felled a 50-foot tree. The tree trunk near its top was more than a foot in diameter and was an impressive obstacle. The three of us jumped out of the car in hopes of lifting the tree to the roadside, but it cruelly snapped back at us with the force of an 18-inch thick rubber band, since it was still attached to the stump. Without a chainsaw, this impediment was going nowhere. Abner was trying to finish me off. His curse was growing stronger, and I firmly believe that someone had recently pillaged his gravesite, causing this burst of spectral strength. If I made it out of the predicament alive, I was going to visit the Arlington National Cemetery in Virginia, kneel down and ask for forgiveness.

Tony said screw it, and drove over the tree. Take that, Abner.

Sure, it continued to rain all night, but Sunday turned out okay. The induction ceremonies went off without incident, so I suppose Abner took a break and had pity upon Bruce Sutter. Or maybe it was because I had already left Cooperstown.

I was on my way to Syracuse for a minor league game with my friend, Suzie. We had a great time and each got a good laugh from an old man taking tickets at the gate. She was wearing a t-shirt that had

"I Love Summer" emblazoned across her chest. When she handed him her ticket, he ripped it and eyed her bosom, replying only to her chest, "I love summer, too."

So do I. Summer is a great time for everything baseball, even if Abner Doubleday and his powerful curse wreak havoc year after year. In the final exhausting moments of Induction Weekend 2006, everything seemed resolved and peaceful, mimicking the end of a hundred slasher films. Alas, like those horror movies, the peace is very likely fleeting. I picture myself like a character who somehow survived two hours of gore, lounging out on the lake. All is right with the world until a ravaged corpse emerges from its watery grave and drags me into the water for a final shocking death. I guess I'll have to wait until 2007 to see if Abner's Curse has yet another sequel.

I Want to Be a Fireman
When I Grow Up

The first baseball game I can remember watching was the infamous "Pine Tar Game" involving the Kansas City Royals and New York Yankees in 1983. It probably wasn't the first game I watched, but it is the first one I remember. My father was a Yankees fan so I, too, was inclined to like the Yankees when I was a kid, but I didn't really attach myself to any of those specific players from that early-80s team. I did know that I disliked George Brett. During that game, he seemed a little scary. As time wore on, I ended up liking Brett and hating the Yankees. It's kind of like bologna and tomatoes. As a child, I could eat bologna sandwiches at every meal, but I wouldn't touch a tomato. Now, I appreciate the taste of tomatoes and I know that bologna has enough unnatural fillers and sodium in it to kill you. Your tastes just change.

In the first few years, my early baseball idols made no sense. Living in northern New York, the only games I ever saw live were the pick up games in my back yard and the only ones on television involved the Yankees. I never even had the opportunity to watch New York Met games until 1985 or 1986. Because of all of the baseball information I consumed through the newspapers, books and the backs of baseball cards, though, I felt I had a connection with a number of players. Dale Murphy, the two-time MVP of the National League, was my first favorite player, despite the fact that I never witnessed him patrolling centerfield until two or three years after I first started watching baseball. My favorite American League player was Fred Lynn, basically because he was on the cover of a *Sports Illustrated* in 1985 when he joined the Baltimore Orioles. By that point, I had watched a few dozen American League games not involving the Yankees, thanks to weekend broadcasts on the major television stations. I still can't remember Lynn, though.

Those memories obviously still resonate with me today, and when I checked the promotions schedule of the Rochester Red Wings early in 2006, I noticed that a "Fred Lynn" day was coming in early August. The chance to meet one of my childhood idols was certainly a draw, even if it was a lengthy drive the night before I would be trekking to New England for a few games.

Prior to Fred Lynn night, I had seen only two games in Rochester. One was my first-ever minor league game in 2001. Rain washed out a pair of collegiate playoff games I was supposed to work in Brockport, but the weather was good enough for a night game at Frontier Field. It's a beautiful park, one of the best in the International League. Trains go by in the outfield (it seems every park in New York has a love affair with trains), there are two good-sized scoreboards, the dugouts are huge with plenty of room on each side for fans to gawk at the players, and the outside is built out of brick, making for a very attractive stadium.

I arrived very early for the game, a good 20 minutes prior to the gates opening, but what I saw outside horrified me. Apparently Fred Lynn enjoyed quite a post-career following since there was a pair of lines that stretched several hundred feet beyond the gates. Once the gates opened, things moved slowly, but I didn't fret. I figured that not all of these people could possibly be here just to see Lynn and the line would move quickly.

Was I ever wrong.

The line to meet Lynn, who I couldn't even see thanks to the winding picket fence set up to corral the autograph seekers, was as lengthy as it had been outside. Several hundred feet separated Lynn and me. After five minutes, an usher came down and announced that Mr. Lynn would be signing autographs until 10 minutes before the start of the game and not everyone was guaranteed to receive an autograph. My innards bubbled up in a fury. I stood in the line for about 20 minutes and moved about 15 feet forward in those 20 minutes, but most of that was likely due to my pacing. I possess incredible patience in all but two arenas: driving and waiting behind other people in a line. My anger consumed me and because of that consumption I grew hungry. I dropped out of the line, wished the people behind me luck, and went into the stadium to sit down and collect my thoughts.

It's difficult to comprehend, but I was really troubled by that line. Sure, Fred Lynn was a childhood idol of mine, but I rarely saw him play on television and never in person. So why was I so irritated? I guess it's no different than looking at pictures of celebrities and seeing their eyes. You think they are looking right back at you and they are excited to meet *you*. That connection I had with Fred Lynn when I was nine years old was still there as I recalled the picture of Lynn with a bat on his shoulder on the *Sports Illustrated* cover staring back at me. The caption read, "Have Bat, Will Travel." I haven't seen that cover in 20 years, but I remember every detail of Lynn's face and the Orioles jersey he sported. I don't think Lynn would recall much about the cover or the story, unless it is framed somewhere in his house with countless other pieces of memorabilia. He was probably too busy getting in shape for the 1985 season.

With several thousand more fans than I was used to, I decided not to sit in my front-row seat down the third base line. The place was just too crowded and I was no longer in the mood, so I headed out beyond the left field wall into a picnic area to watch the game. There, the Pawtucket bullpen was in full view of the fans. I watched a couple players screw around and locate their perches on the bench for the next few innings. The visitors' bullpen at Rochester is above field level, but also sunken below the concourse, allowing any passersby to watch the pitchers warm up. The bullpen was like a fishbowl and every fan gawking and talking to the pitchers while they tried to prepare for their jobs was some idiot at the pet store tapping on the glass.

The biggest fish in the bowl was Keith Foulke, who was finishing up his rehabilitation with the Paw Sox. He was down by the dugout during pre-game talking with reporters, while fans accosted him at every opportunity. He signed numerous autographs for Red Sox fans and others while I passively looked on because it took me a good three or four minutes to figure out who he was. Talk about non-descript looking: I'm sure if I still lived in Boston I would have recognized the guy who helped deliver the Red Sox their World Series Championship in 2004. In Rochester, however, I was oblivious.

Out in left field with the boys in the bullpen, I felt a little more at peace watching the ballgame. My irritation regarding the Fred Lynn situation was beginning to subside. It wasn't so much my thought process that allowed for the cool down, as it was the antics of the relief pitchers. While kids and teenagers pestered the relievers for free baseballs, autographs, gloves, cleats, socks, rosin bags, and anything else that wasn't nailed down, I enjoyed the banter. Tim Bausher, a 27-year-old righty, pulled his pant legs up above his knee caps, showing four inches of skin between his high socks and thighs and waltzed around the mounds in a sort of "hi, fellas!" nerdish way. Bausher clearly was one of the clowns of the bullpen, something that each and every reliever corps needs. Functioning as a relief pitcher is the kind of job that you have to keep light prior to the game because once a reliever is called upon, the game is likely in jeopardy and seriousness and focus are vital. In the first few innings, though, anything goes.

A few innings later, an older teenager, probably a high school upper classman, approached the railing above the bullpen. He was wearing Yankees gear, and appeared ready to taunt the group with some sophisticated comments, as most Yankees' fans are prone to do. However, he held back and asked Bausher a question.

"Is that Wakefield?" the teen asked.

"That's him down there," Bausher pointed.

"Which one?" the teen replied.

"The one in the red," Bausher said. Fellow reliever Jermaine Van Buren, a 6-1, 220-pound African-American is only 26 years old. Tim Wakefield is a 40-year-old white knuckleball pitcher. All the while Van Buren didn't crack a smile, probably because he wasn't listening to the conversation. Since Van Buren seemed somewhat gregarious in Ottawa when Dave Trombley was throwing umpires out of a game in early May, I'm sure he could have hardly kept a straight face had he heard Bausher toying with this poor fan.

"That's not Wakefield," responded the incredulous Yankee fan.

"Yeah, it is," said Bausher.

"No, it's not," fired back the teen.

"Yeah, it is," Bausher repeated.

"Tim Wakefield *isn't* black," the teen said, ending the conversation with Bausher.

"Why would Wakefield be here?" asked Keith Foulke.

"Cuz, he's hurt," replied the Yankee fan.

"He has a broken rib! He'll be out for a while," Foulke said.

The fishbowl was just beginning to rock back and forth from all of the glass tapping.

Despite the annoying fans glaring down from above, the whole situation helped me recall the times when I was a kid playing in Little League. In the summer after 4th grade, I remember coming in to pitch during the league's championship game and pitching the final two innings to get a save. It was a big deal to me at the time, obviously, but it was especially glorious to earn a save because I had moved past Fred Lynn as one of my favorites to lefty reliever Dave Righetti of the New York Yankees. Righetti was on his way to setting a new mark for saves in a season, recording 46 that year. I had a glove with his name in it and I spent hours near the high school throwing a baseball against an 8-by-20 foot brick wall that was meant to be a practice area for soccer goalies. Every morning during the summer, I would pretend I was Dave Righetti (suddenly right-handed), and fantasize about striking out the side in the ninth inning, identifying a certain area in the bricks as a strike zone. I always seemed to retire the side without ever being touched, which is what happened in that league championship game. I knew Righetti would be proud. Of course, these guys in the bullpen, outside of Foulke and Marc Deschenes, were all younger than me, so they probably spent their time imagining Bobby Thigpen, Dennis Eckersley or Rob Dibble. Hopefully, their arms matched up with their idols.

I loved pitching in relief when I was younger. Relievers reminded me of bullfighters, coming out of the gates to the roar of applause and adulation with pressure surrounding them. Relievers simply had to avoid giving up runs and losing the game, while bullfighters had to avoid the horns and strong muscles of bulls to keep their limbs. Either way, the jobs were the same: avoid the hazards and finish as a conquering hero.

Apparently in Rochester there are more hazards than batters and base runners. In Rochester, you have to make sure that the fishbowl isn't toppled. While Foulke's explanation of why Jermaine Van Buren was not Tim Wakefield pacified one fan for a few minutes, a fresh crew of kids sidled up to the railing and riddled Foulke with questions. He ignored the kids for about five minutes, but finally he snapped.

"Hey, Mr. Foulke?" one said.

"What!?" Foulke shouted back. It wasn't so much of an angry shout as it was an "I'm fed up with this constant badgering…what the hell do you want so I can get on with my life?" shout.

"Can I have a ball?"

"Do you know David Ortiz?"

"Can I have your hat?"

"Do you know Manny Ramirez?"

"Can I have your glove?"

"Do you know Curt Schilling?"

"Can I have your cleats?"

"When are you going back to the Red Sox?"

"Can I have the rosin bag?"

"Are you mad that Papelbon took your job?"

Foulke dutifully answered the silly questions from the kids for about 10 minutes, skipping the occasional question as he saw fit and waiting for the next rapid fire shot while pacing the bullpen mounds and manicuring the bullpen grass. He stopped the conversations when a drop-dead gorgeous blonde closed in on the rail. She looked to be in her mid-30s, wore some expensive high-heeled shoes, was casually well-dressed and did not look like she should be at a minor league baseball game. I quickly deduced that this was Foulke's wife.

He sent his head to the side to convey to her she should walk to the other end of the bullpen behind the advertisement boards so their conversation could be private. She complied and clip-clopped herself behind the boards to have a moment with her husband. Every male head in the picnic area followed her path and for the next 10 minutes every male head occasionally spun itself over to the spot where she had disappeared, waiting for her to return.

What's not to love about being a relief pitcher? Play and watch baseball every day during the spring and summer. Check. Make fun of fans and chew gum or sunflower seeds for five or six innings. Check. Throw a few pitches and receive glory and money. Check. Date or marry hot women. Check.

I took a wrong turn in life somewhere.

Adoration by Association

By mid-August, Joshua Papelbon was a celebrity in New England. He was among the league leaders in saves, relief earned run average, and strikeouts per nine innings. Every time he emerged from the home dugout, kids screamed for his autograph and adults wearing Boston Red Sox paraphernalia wanted to shake his hand and congratulate him on his success.

Such is the life as a member of the Lowell Spinners, Boston's New York-Penn League affiliate, located just 30 miles from Fenway Park. Especially if your big brother, Jonathan, is a top candidate for Rookie of the Year, and among the leaders in the American League in saves, relief earned run average, and strikeouts per nine innings.

I noticed this phenomenon the first time I saw Lowell back in early July in Vermont. The Lake Monsters are an affiliate of the Washington Nationals, but a large portion of the fans in Vermont claim to be fans of the Red Sox. There was a buzz in the crowd that day when the side-winding, relief-pitching brother of Jonathan Papelbon was right there in front of them. It's not like their last name is Smith or Jones, and Joshua Papelbon could just pass by incognito. Even a keen-eyed novice fan could pick that name out and put two and two together.

Normally, it would be a lot of pressure for a kid with such lineage; everyone predicting that you, too, will come in out of the bullpen and blow 95-mile-per-hour heat past every hitter you face and then sauntering back to the dugout as the hero of the day. However, Joshua Papelbon was selected in the 48th round out of North Florida in the 2006 major league draft and not much of anything is expected of 48th round draft picks other than filling a roster spot at the lower levels. After a year or two, many of these draft picks find themselves back in the real world.

Joshua Papelbon was making the most of his opportunity, even if he likely was a nepotism pick. In 15 games, Papelbon saved seven and struck out 19 while walking only two in 17 innings of work to post a 2.08 ERA, and Lowell loved him for it. Meanwhile, T.J. Large, a Lowell relief pitcher without the benefit of a big brother in the major leagues, puttered along unnoticed with seven saves, 32 strikeouts against eight walks in 28 innings. When he popped out of the dugout, a few fans requested his autograph, but he begged off. He had to drive the grounds crew's gator off to safety.

Some other notes from Lowell:

1) There is a psycho hot dog vendor in New England. It seems every minor league team has at least one "character" vendor in its park, but they even put this guy on the video scoreboard, belting out the chorus of "Who Let the Dogs Out," followed by the crowd barking, a played-out call in stadiums across the world. The vendor is in his late-50s at least, but it was hard to nail down his age because of a long gray beard that resembled the late Jerry Garcia's of the Grateful Dead. He kind of looked like a homeless war veteran. It made me wonder if there is some sort of unwritten minor league rule that requires every organization to hire a relatively harmless homeless person to work in its stadium as a way of giving back to the city. I'm going to search the fine print in the professional baseball agreement and all minor league charters.

2) A favorite pastime of many stadiums is also the bane of human existence: the chicken dance. When this hell-sent abomination was released on the conforming public, it should have come with the caveat that senior citizens and kids, who lack the coordination for actual dancing, are the only ones allowed to perform it. Anyone else caught doing this dance should be shunned from society and placed on an isle for criminals similar to the way the British used Australia a few centuries ago. Anyway, along with the horrific atrocity that is

the chicken dance, the Lowell Spinners were simultaneously chucking rubber chickens into the crowd. Standing only a few feet away from the stands, an intern ran past with a chicken for tossing. He then violently whirled his arm in a softball style motion and accidentally threw the rubber souvenir at about 90 miles per hour directly into the chest of a fan sitting in the front row. I have a feeling that this does not come under the standard warning given before each game reminding fans that the ballclub is not responsible for injuries suffered during the game when bats and balls can fly unexpectedly into the stands; while you may be sitting in foul territory, it may or may not be fowl territory.

Svengali

Words can confuse people, sometimes intentionally. Other times the listener or reader interprets only a portion of the information prior to the completion of the story. It's a slippery slope as both a writer and storyteller. Being someone who is very capable of compiling a tale that is both outrageous and believable off the top of my head while maintaining a straight face, this has allowed me the opportunity to pull off some beautifully constructed lies. It is interesting to watch the stretch of human emotion alter before your very eyes, seeing my victim's face fall from wide-eyed amazement to a broken and sullen stare. I've done it for years and will continue to do so. Call it a hobby.

There are also many times when my stories are just misconstrued. When I tell people that I've met certain ballplayers and can reveal to them interesting anecdotes about some players' lives, they have no idea that the meeting took place with a wall between the two of us and the anecdotes are sometimes pulled from reading materials. I'm really not trying to mislead anyone. When I told a girl a few years younger than me at a game in Portland, Maine, that I had met New York Mets third baseman David Wright, she immediately pulled out a business card for me to give to him.

"No, I met him a couple years ago in Binghamton and then saw him a few other places," I explained.

"Well, I usually don't do this, but he is really good looking and I'd like a chance to meet him," she responded, not listening to my statement.

"You don't understand, I don't have his cell phone number or his email, I simply met him a couple times in 2004 when he was in the minor leagues," I said.

"Oh," she said, drawn out. "Well, next time you talk to him give this to him for me, will you?"

I snatched the card from her hand, murmured the words, "All right," and walked away, discarding the card in the nearest trash receptacle. I met David Wright in Binghamton in 2004 while he was with the B-Mets and he truly is a great guy. It's not like we sat down for coffee and a sandwich at some bistro and discussed the world's problems. Every time I went to a game that Wright played in, I made a point to try and talk to him, knowing full well that it would only be a matter of time before he was playing with the real Mets. I saw him all over the minors in both Double-A and Triple-A, ending the routine just a week or so before his promotion to the major leagues. Just a few minutes prior to a game in Ottawa when he was playing for the Norfolk Tides, I requested his company near the corner of the first base dugout and dropped a handful of tickets down on top of its roof, asking for him to sign the stubs for the sake of posterity.

"Wow," he said. "Are all these games from this year?"

"Yeah," I came back, glad that he didn't recognize me as a stalker, just as a fan of his. "I know there's a bunch of them, but would you mind signing them for me?"

"Sure," he responded, dutifully picking up my pen and affixing his signature across a half-dozen ticket stubs. Wright is a notoriously good signer and in the few times that I saw him play, he almost always immediately came over to the railing to initiate conversation with both adults and kids, often taking small children in his arms to pose for pictures. He normally would place his glove on top of his head like a kid, assuring that he would never leave it behind, just in case his mother heard about it and sent him back outside to find it.

"You know, David, just about every time I've seen you play this year, you've gone like 3-for-4 with a home run or 4-for-5 with a couple doubles or something," I said while he finished off the last ticket.

"Really?" he asked. "Geez, I should give you my tickets for every game. Enjoy the game today." He finished the statement and jogged back into the dugout waving goodbye to me just moments before the umpires came out to start the game.*

This is what I mean by having "met" certain ballplayers. I can't pull out my cell phone and text message David Wright to ask him if he wants to go clubbing in Manhattan. After I have talked to a ballplayer a few times, I usually can conclude that I have an idea of what kind of person he is. Most are fairly relaxed before games, and the outgoing players will enjoy some banter with the fans if they have something in common. I know enough about most players that I usually can come up with something semi-intelligible and I've learned that if there is nothing to say, don't bother with anything at all. It's not like I just start spouting off about my life with every person I meet.

Unfortunately, that's not everyone's theory on the subject.

After tossing out the business card of some delirious floozy who wanted to jump in line to be the next Mrs. Wright, I found myself standing next to an older woman leaning against a fence near the clubhouse at Hadlock Field. It was about 75 minutes prior to game time in Portland, whose ballpark tries to mirror Boston's Fenway Park with a smaller seating capacity. Portland's fans also try to mirror the hometown feel of "our" guys that Red Sox fans seem to embrace despite the increased separation between the players and the general public.

"You waiting for anyone special?" asked the older lady. We had stood in silence for five minutes before she startled me with a question normally reserved for a female groupie. The tone wasn't

---

* *I've seen Wright play a few more times in the major leagues since then, but my statement was true then and it still is. In the 11 games that I've watched Wright in person, he has batted .409 with two home runs, six doubles and 11 RBI, slugging .682 with an on-base percentage of .447. Of course, that day in Ottawa he naturally went 0-for-5 with three strikeouts, ending any chance of me earning his daily allotment of tickets for the next 15 years.*

harsh, but her voice wasn't quite the sweet sound I expected to flow from her aged mouth. No lint covered butterscotch candies would be emerging from the bottom of her purse for me.

"Jacoby Ellsbury," I responded. "He's a good young player. I met him a couple times last year when he was with Lowell. He seems like a pretty nice kid."

"Eh," she said, her head turning towards the fence in disgust. "He's kind of standoffish."

"Really?" I came back. "I didn't find that at all."

"Well, you know those guys who get drafted higher, their agents tell them when they get up in the higher levels, especially Double-A and Triple-A, that they don't have to stop and sign autographs any more or talk to anybody."

"Really?"

"Oh, yes."

"Huh."

The older lady continued on, telling me that over the past decade or so she has become a bit of a surrogate grandmother for the young players going through Portland, cooking meals for them and making them feel at home in a strange place. She bragged about how she had seen just about every big star in the major leagues come through Portland, and that she could remember them before they were anything special in the big leagues. She also unburdened herself telling of the awful sight of seeing a guy "let all of the big league stuff get to his head when he was here a few weeks ago."

"Who was that?" I asked, not recalling any major league players going through Portland recently.

"Oh, I don't want to say his name," she responded.

"It's okay, it's not like I'm going to tell on you," I kidded her. She didn't get the joke.

"Well, I'm not afraid of you telling on me," she snapped, her bitterness boiling over. "He just complained that the cement from here to the clubhouse was going to ruin his spikes and he demanded that they put carpet down."

"Really?" Each one of my single-word responses sounded more and more incredulous.

"Oh, yes," she said. "Demanded carpet!"

Was this woman trying to play my own game against me? I have to admit, looking down at the imperfect blacktop, the story sounded like it could be somewhat true, but why would anyone complain about concrete and spikes?

"Well, aren't the dugout floors here and everywhere else made of concrete?" I asked rhetorically. "Or are they flush will rose petals at Fenway Park?"

She didn't like that joke, either.

"All I know is that he *demanded* carpet!"

She clearly was getting upset so I decided not to push it any further. Besides, Ellsbury was coming out of the home clubhouse and I wanted to talk to him. I called him over, he stopped, we chatted for a minute (I congratulated him on his alma mater, Oregon State, winning the NCAA National Championship in baseball), and he left for the field. One guess to who now had the incredulous look on her face.

"Wow, I've only seen him stop over once before," she said. "Do you really know him?"

I felt a need to toy with her for a few moments after all of the bullshit she was spewing from her lips, but my cell phone rang. I hoisted it out of my cargo shorts' pocket and looked at the number. The call was from my friend, Mike, but I just couldn't help myself.

"Sorry, David Wright is calling me," I said with a straight face. "I've got to take this."

Roll Back in the Standings

Upon meeting someone for the first time, the acquaintance usually asks to what team I pledge my allegiance. An expression of disbelief often covers the person's face when I tell them that not only do I not root for the New York Yankees, but I actively root against them and have particular favor for the team that defeats them in the post-season the previous year. Some refer to me as a "hater." I refer to myself as someone who roots against Satan.

A lot has been written about the "evil empire" over the past few years, especially with the Red Sox-Yankees rivalry renewing itself with the fervor of the pre-Reagan levels and even surpassing it in terms of money and bickering. Several writers far superior to me have written ad nauseam about how rooting for the Yankees is like rooting for US Steel or other dominating conglomerates. A few generations ago that was an excellent correlation, but I've come to the conclusion that the Yankees are the baseball equivalent to Wal-Mart.

I have nothing against Wal-Mart. In fact, I like to go there to buy everyday items, such as picture frames, sport drinks, the occasional movie, or even soap. It's a one-stop shopping Mecca. That explained, the proliferation of the franchise is at the heart of the destruction of modern society and its inability to focus. At one point in history, mini-malls seemed to unravel the fabric of downtown shopping and specialty stores in quaint little villages. Everything was inside, the stores were right next to one another, you could easily run to a food court for a bite to eat and, if you were under the age of 12 or a nerd, a video arcade was just around the corner. Wal-Mart stepped up the show by eliminating the walls and buying in so much bulk that the prices dropped to microscopic levels. Initially this is great for the consumer, but it becomes too easy and our imagination is eliminated. Without the craftsmanship of a true artisan, the consumer forgets what quality looks like and disregards the hard-earned knowledge and experience that a craftsman takes years to acquire.

That's what the New York Yankees and its fans resemble: Wal-Mart and its customers. They have no patience and no imagination. Rebuild the team and just start with a solid nucleus of players? Blasphemy! Just go out and buy the best players (Wal-Mart equivalent of lowering prices so that the mom-and-pop store can't possibly survive since they do not possess the capability of suffering a brief loss) once they reach free agency and take another run at the trophy. I would think that being a Yankees fan would be rather joyless. Knowing that your team is going to be good year after year is easy and sucks out all of the imagination and hope that is inherent in all sports. Know anyone who is happy all the time? Probably not. But if you do, it's someone who you regard as an idiot or flake. Sports, like any person with numerous emotions and characteristics, should be filled with ups and downs to make the human experience that much more memorable. Sure, it's wonderful to have "one of those days" where everything goes well. When that happens, the elation is pure. If you have "one of those days" every day, than it ceases to be "one of those days" and become every day. This is why people do drugs, to try and find new highs. I really can't comprehend how anyone can want to root for that team or feel good about themselves while doing it. If the Yankees were some sort of model of ingenuity in which the team simply rebuilt itself from the inside out every few years without missing a beat, that's one thing. To simply pick up the stars of other organizations to create a bigger behemoth is unfair and unimaginative.

Hatred for the New York team aside, I bought tickets to sit in the bleachers at Yankee Stadium. Cleveland and its hodgepodge of fans would pale in comparison. As far as I was concerned, the bleacher sections of Yankee Stadium were the demilitarized zone of baseball. Korea's 38th parallel-DMZ is one of the only places in the world, along with anything involving Israel, with more potential violence on any given day. The stories passed back and forth from attendees sound like the utterances of war veterans from conflicts gone past. Swearing, off-color remarks, filth and untethered enthusiasm for the empire of evil fill the air.

How could I pass all that up?

I purchased a pair of tickets for a Sunday game in August with the Los Angeles Angels of Anaheim (for now on referred to as Anaheim, because I think their name is incredibly lame and better suited for a fantasy team) against the Yankees. Surprisingly, it was very difficult to find someone to attend the game with me. Perhaps all of my friends feared for their safety. At the last second, I convinced my friend Hillary to take a train down from Schenectady to see the game with me. She had never been to Yankee Stadium, so she was justifiably excited to go. I had attended a game at the stadium two years prior to this one, so I was just happy to see a game between two decent teams with playoff hopes. The first time I went to Yankee Stadium, I was not filled with awe or struck with some sort of life epiphany the way it is described by every hack writer on earth. Yes, many great players have jogged around the bases in historical games at Yankee Stadium. They also did at Busch Stadium, Fenway Park, Wrigley Field, and Dodger Stadium. What will those same fans say a few years from now when they move into the new ballpark? Will they call it "The House that $800 Million of YES Network Revenue Built?"

When Hillary and I met outside the ballpark, I handed her the ticket that was sent to me through the mail when I purchased it from Ebay. Printed boldly across the ticket were the words "Pride, Power, Pinstripes." I felt ill. "Pricks, Pox, Plaid" would have rung better in my ears.

Things got better once we went inside. It was a beautiful day and not too hot, ranging somewhere in the mid-70s with a blue sky. I still feared sunburn, so I purchased (gulp) a Yankees hat to cover my head from the sun. Admittedly, it was a pretty nice hat, but as soon as I signed the credit card receipt I came to the conclusion that the chapeau would become my father's lid the next time I made my way through my parents' door. Along with the Yankees cap, I continued to look the part in wearing my Thurman Munson Cooperstown Collection jersey. When you are about to walk through hell, you don't cover yourself in gasoline, oil, or any other accelerant.

I tried not to cheer openly when the Anaheim leadoff hitter, Chone Figgins, homered on the second pitch of the game. Or when Howie Kendrick singled. Or when Orlando Cabrera singled. Or when Juan Rivera drove in a run with another single. Or when Adam Kennedy drove in a third run with another single. With a gaunt Phil Rizzuto impersonator sitting next to me (I don't know, maybe it was Phil) and hundreds of other Yankee supporters surrounding me, I didn't think this was the time to gloat. New York starter Chien-Ming Wang was sure to settle down and, although unbeaten rookie pitcher Jered Weaver was on the hill for Anaheim, I wasn't quite ready to call the game over after the top of the first inning.

Everyone's least favorite Yankee, Alex Rodriguez, was struggling through a slump and struck out swinging in the first inning, but he shouldn't have felt bad since no one touched Weaver in the first, save for a walk from Derek Jeter; Johnny Damon and Bobby Abreu also flailed at strike three in the first. Unfortunately it took Weaver 26 pitches to do it, which is never a good sign at Yankee Stadium.

The innings passed along without any upheaval in the stands, a shocking development considering the team fell behind early. Weaver was mowing through the Yankee lineup without too much difficulty, allowing only a single hit in the first four innings. The top of the fifth saw the Angels score a fourth run with another RBI-single from Juan Rivera (a former New York prospect). The Yankees got on the scoreboard in the bottom of the inning when newcomer Craig Wilson dropped a bomb in to the left field stands to make the score 4-1. The Angels added another run in the sixth when Kendrick singled home Curtis Pride. Even trailing by four runs, nothing was happening in the stands.

I was disappointed. One game is hardly enough to make any kind of definitive statement about a ballpark or its fans, but from the tales

I had heard I expected *something* to happen; a fistfight, someone pouring a soda on another fan, a mugging, a bee sting, *anything*. Then right around the seventh inning stretch, it happened.

The two teams were not even playing one another yet. Sure, the abnormal five-game series was coming up in a few days, and I can understand why a fan would want to support his team, but why, *oh why*, would you wear your Boston Red Sox hat and jersey in the Yankee Stadium bleachers on a sold-out Sunday afternoon game with absolutely no help in sight? The idiot made his way to his seat as hundreds of eyes stared daggers at his jersey. In New York, there was no way it could possibly stop there. Garbage came flying in, f-bombs dropped, and open ridicule ensued.

But it got much worse. As the Yankee fans' surrounding circle gained depth, density and proximity to the lone Red Sox supporter, his once daring conduct diminished as he appeared fearful of a stoning reprisal for the 2004 American League Championship Series. The standing fans began to wave out as everyone rose out of their seats to see what was happening (I wonder if this is how the first celebratory wave began in Seattle over a quarter of a century ago. Had a Denver Broncos fan dared to wear a Craig Morton jersey at the Kingdome?). I, too, became caught in the moment, not to join in, but to watch the sociological display unfold before me. A full section away, my view was far from clear, but I never saw the Red Sox fan again. The combined mental powers of the Yankee fans might have created a vacuum in which the Sox fan simply ceased to exist, his molecules disintegrating or imploding, but I figured that would likely make some kind of noise. Besides, the combined mental powers of the Yankee fans in the bleachers couldn't warm a pop tart, let alone cause a body to implode.

The ninth inning rolled around with the Angels still up 5-1. Jeter and Abreu struck out to open the inning, but the gritty, gutsy Alex Rodriguez came through with a solo home run to cut the lead to 5-2. As soon as the ball left the bat and sailed through the outfield towards the fence, I murmured "typical" under my breath, knowing that my father, watching the game several hundred miles away was either saying the same thing or laughing aloud at the "clutch" hit from A-

Rod. Another home run followed from Jason Giambi and the Angels decided to take the game seriously by bringing in Francisco Rodriguez, who promptly shut the door and ended the contest with the Angels claiming a 5-3 victory.

Hillary and I shuffled out with the rest of the crowd to the parking garage with zero hope of leaving the premises any time in the near future, thanks to an ungodly amount of traffic. New York lost, but I was nonetheless disappointed in the game after being led astray by the stories of the Yankee Stadium bleachers. My expectations were certainly high, perhaps even unrealistic since anything short of a public hanging would have been marked as a let down. Other than the questionable disappearance of a Red Sox supporter, the New York fans had behaved throughout the contest, cheering their own and giving only good natured ribbing to the opposition. Even the ushers and ticket takers bid us goodbye with smiles and, "We'll get 'em next time" looks on their faces. After all of these years, have I been a victim of anti-New York bias by jealous sportswriters? Have I simply become too jaded by the Yankees consistent winning? Have I been too harsh regarding owner George Steinbrenner, the Yankees, and their fan base who spend 81 games genuflecting at the turnstiles of the "House that Ruth Built?"

Nah. I'm far from a Shakespearean scholar, but I believe a certain speech from Antonio in Act 1, Scene 3 of "The Merchant of Venice" best describes the situation:

"Mark you this, Bassanio,
The devil can cite Scripture for his purpose.
An evil soul producing holy witness
Is like a villain with a smiling cheek,
A goodly apple rotten at the heart:
O, what a goodly outside falsehood hath!"

Having written such a statement more than four centuries ago, Shakespeare would have served as an ideal prophet for Boston Red Sox owner Harry Frazee while he was dealing with New York owners Jacob Ruppert and Cap Huston in a certain transaction involving one George Herman Ruth. Perhaps he could have changed the course of history. Frazee would have listened. After all, he did love the theatre.*

* *For those unfamiliar: Babe Ruth was just at the beginning of his memorable career as a hitter when Boston owner Harry Frazee sold him to the Yankees for $125,000 and a $300,000 loan, putting up Fenway Park as collateral, all to help finance his Broadway endeavors.*

Auburn Will Hate Me

I'm going straight to hell. Throughout this book I have occasionally mocked towns, stadiums, and fans, but this section will surpass ridicule and border upon cruelty. However, it's not totally my fault.

In 2005, my friend Pittsy and I attended a game at Falcon Park in Auburn, NY. We spent a fair amount of time walking around the modest stadium, which seats around 3,000 patrons, and he noticed one undeniable fact: this was one unattractive crowd. I laughed, looked around, and backed up his statement. There would be no Calvin Klein models coming from the Doubledays' fan base on this day. On repeated visits to Auburn, the crowd didn't change much, and it certainly didn't get any prettier. The occasional good-looking 17-year-old would walk by, but it would never last.

Auburn's fan base helped me arrive at a theory across the minor leagues. Although there are certainly aberrations which don't always fit my hypothesis, I've come to the conclusion that the lower the level in the minor leagues, the more unsightly the crowd. Part of this could be that the lower levels generally aren't in larger markets, which doesn't allow for a deepening of the gene pool, but even the small cities which have Low A and High A franchises don't always draw attractive fans.

Now that I've written all of this, feel free to send hate mail, Auburn, NY. Just remember, I never noticed it before my friend Pittsy so astutely pointed it out. I only came up with the theory. I can't even imagine what happens in Rookie ball. Fans there must be crawling out of the primordial evolutionary muck.

Hurricane Ernesto brought a deluge to New York during the first weekend of September, which actually worked to my benefit. In the first few days of September, I had already planned on watching a game in Auburn in the afternoon and then driving the 30 miles to Syracuse to see a Sky Chiefs game. The rain brought by Ernesto forced a traditional doubleheader onto the Auburn schedule, as the Doubledays would take on Williamsport. I was very appreciative of Mother Nature on this one, because the misty rain was just enough to keep the walk up crowd to a minimum, yet it allowed those with planned trips to go ahead and attend.

My friend Scott and I pulled in around 12:15, only to find out the field wouldn't be ready until 1:30, which was all right since he had never been to Auburn before and he wanted to explore the stadium a bit. When the game finally did begin around 1:30, we decided to sit directly behind the plate in the general admission section, which can't be more than 150 feet from the mound.

As the first pitch was thrown, a throng of pitchers came out in street clothes to chart the game. Apparently the Williamsport Crosscutters decided that they needed to know what the wind speed was at the time of every pitch because six guys came out with clipboards. I think I would find that intimidating on two different fronts. If I was charting for the other team, I would feel outnumbered and perhaps a little inferior, questioning my own methods of charting. If I were the starting pitcher for Williamsport, I would feel as though I was being prodded and analyzed to death by my peers and future competition. What if they decided to put together a diabolical sabotage strategy while sitting in the stands and end my career before it could really get started? Paranoid, sure, but remember that some of these guys wouldn't even be playing pro ball the next season. With such great odds against you as a pitcher, can you imagine not being a little wary of conspiracies?

It didn't take long for the crowd to shuffle in behind Scott and me in the metal bleachers behind home plate. Shuffle is the appropriate word, too. The average age of the bunch was 87. This crowd wasn't as ugly as usual, but what they made up for in former beauty was brought back down by gravity. I figured there were a couple reasons why so many older people came out to the ballpark on this day. Perhaps, because it was Sunday, this was routine and they always came to the park after worship. Or maybe they mistook the outer brick building at Falcon Park for a church. Then again, maybe it was a rest home's weekly or monthly outing. Whatever, there were about 50 people sitting in the surrounding sections who were on the downside of post-retirement. I'm not exaggerating. I saw canes, walkers, and wheelchairs. You name the mode of assisted locomotion, I saw it. Ironically, outside the stadium, next to the road separating the park and the parking lot, was a sign reading "Chasing Foul Balls Prohibited." The sign was meant to keep kids from crisscrossing the road because of traffic, but no kids were in sight on this day. This crowd would have struggled to chase down a ball that had rolled to a stop.

I would love to recount the conversations that I heard behind me once the game began, but they were all so nonsensical and incoherent, I couldn't decipher most of them. One elderly man was speaking like Cab Calloway. He seemed to repeat the refrain, "Hidy-hidy-hidy-hi, skiddly-be-bop-de-do-dop," but at about three times the speed it just took to read. It brought me back to the movie, *The Blues Brothers*. Another aged man (at least I think it was a man) looked like an albino version of Sammy Davis, Jr. I've never seen or heard anything like this display in Auburn. Did the active seniors forget to take some medication? Sometime in the fifth inning, one older gentleman decided to belt out "Casey Pogo-Poo," whatever that means. Scott and I looked at each other in sheer joy at the golden nuggets that I was receiving from this non-medicated crowd. "Casey Pogo-Poo" the man screeched again. Where were the caregivers? "Wendell!" another man screeched. "Wendell!" Was Wendell the caregiver? This group was getting out of control, and it was early in the game. An inning later, a guy in his early-60s, one of the young hipsters of the group, started showing off something he clearly had worked on in arts and crafts. It was a cardboard cutout of something resembling a toilet lid with writing in magic marker scribbled everywhere. Lacking only uncooked macaroni pasted around the sides, this piece surely would find its way into the Louvre one day. All of the old people laughed at his antics as well as his childlike illustrations and scissor work. If only I had my camera ready. It said something about "balls" and "peace next season." Considering the guy could barely complete sentences when lured into conversation about his artwork, I'm guessing it was not a political statement.

Despite these raucous characters, there was one interesting man among the gallery. Charlie Wride, who refers to himself as a New York-Penn League historian, happened to be sitting directly behind us as we peered out onto the field of play. Scott was wearing a Jonathan Papelbon jersey he had recently purchased, and the two Red Sox fans struck up a conversation. I kept out of the dialogue, but the two of them seemed to genuinely enjoy one another's banter for a few minutes. Charlie left for a moment, at which point Scott and I enjoyed loud conversations behind us regarding everyone's specific preference between hard shell and soft shell tacos. Thankfully, Charlie returned holding a pair of multi-paged lists that featured all of the active players and coaches who were at one time or another affiliated with the league. He seemed happy to share the information with a pair of baseball fans, showing both pride in his work and in a league he had followed for decades. He even gave Scott his business card, which informed us that Charlie had been watching baseball since 1939. God bless him.

I didn't think much of the lists as Scott passed them over to me between innings. It initially seemed like Charlie was a solitary man who decided to produce a lengthy list of names and their former affiliations with the New York-Penn League and passed those lists out as a mode of bragging, saying, "Look what I've done." On second glance, though, it really was amazing how many great players made their way through the league. It's not like I was unfamiliar with this possibility. Obviously, every current major league player must have competed in some minor league at one point or another, but hundreds of current major leagues were listed, including Cy Young and Most Valuable Player Award winners. Clearly, he had put in a lot of time to document the importance of this specific minor league. Who was I to denigrate his accomplishment?

Besides, to make light of Charlie was like slapping myself in the face. Charlie was me. Or I was Charlie, however you want to look at it. When I was in high school and college, I had graduated from the backs of baseball cards to books discussing my favorite subject. I began poring over the Baseball Encyclopedia day after day, week after week, looking for new information and forming new statistical or biographical lists. Those lists were compiled by hand and written into numerous notebooks before I knew how to turn a computer on. A few years later the lists were typed, once I became unafraid of computers. I remember back in 1997 someone asking me a trivia question about who the last left-handed (throwing) catcher was in the major leagues. I had an idea, but I wasn't absolutely sure, so I went to my encyclopedia and spent the next two hours going through more than 800 pages of players looking for southpaw catchers. I found a handful, wrote them down, and gleefully sent the list off to the trivia master who was dumbfounded by the list when he was only looking for a solitary name from the 1950s (Dale Long, which wasn't, by the way, the correct answer).

Looking down at Charlie's list and remembering those two hours on opening day in 1997, I couldn't help but feel a bit ashamed of how I avoided all eye contact with him when he spoke with Scott. After all, this was a man who had spent nearly 70 years watching baseball's history unfold before his eyes. I was jealous of what he had seen, but I bet he was equally jealous of what Scott and I might see in the future when he was gone. It's amazing how something as simple as the game of baseball can bring people together. Right then, I realized that I had been way too hard on Auburn. It was a quaint little stadium; the people dressed in lots of Auburn Doubledays paraphernalia and couldn't be more proud of the tradition of baseball in the city. I wanted to turn around and apologize to everyone who had heard me murmur any snide comments.

But then "Casey Pogo-Poo" loudly announced to his friend next to him (and unintentionally to two sections around him) that his doctor told him he was no longer able to eat white bread. In case not everyone caught his announcement, he repeated it. "Yup, no more white bread for me. That's what the doctor said."

154

I guess for every Charlie Wride in Auburn, there's at least one "Casey Pogo-Poo." It's a trade off I'm willing to accept.

Hi, My Name Is Tommy And I'm a Baseballaholic (Hi Tommy)

They were hardly the words I expected to continually repeat to myself aloud at 6 p.m.

In the previous 14 hours, I endured waking up at an unimaginable hour to shower. That was followed by two hours of sitting in an airport, a two-hour flight to Detroit, another hour layover, and then a four-hour flight to Phoenix. Forty-five minutes passed before my lone leather bag came tumbling down the baggage claim ramp.

The Phoenix airport has a feel of urban sprawl, so a bus picked me up at the terminal to carry me to the rental car depot. Stumbling through the automatic doors at the rental station, I was accosted by William, the car rental attendant. He was just being friendly, but I was restless after a long flight.

"So what brings you out to Phoenix," he asked with a slight Mexican accent.

"I'm here to watch some baseball games in the Arizona Fall League," I responded, dutifully.

"Business or pleasure?" he retorted.

About twice a year in my travels, I decide to play with someone. William at the counter was one of this year's recipients. "Business," I responded.

A few moments went by before William decided to dig deeper. He already had me flustered and asked what kind of insurance coverage I wanted. "Basic?"

"Uh, yeah, just basic," I said. Silly me, I thought it was going to be $4.99 a day. Lesson learned.

"So what do you do? Are you a scout or a writer?" he asked.

"I'm a writer." It was a true statement, but then the lies started flying. I just wanted a god damn car.

"For a newspaper?" William asked, continuing his examination.

"Yes."

"What's it called?" he asked.

I wanted to yell at him, "Holy shit, Will, just give me the freakin' car!" But I held off.

"American Baseball," I responded, mashing the two-word title of the well-known minor league magazine, *Baseball America*. We continued the conversation for another two minutes as I provided some details concerning my life as a fictitious magazine writer, which I couldn't possibly remember now since the banter went so quickly.

Three years prior to this encounter, I met a man in Winston-Salem who thought he recognized me as a beat writer for the Wake Forest baseball team. The difference was that I had him going for well over a half hour before I decided to duck out, excusing myself to the clubhouses to conduct my post-game interviews. He had started pointing me out to some of his friends and I thought the jig was up. While in Vermont a few months later, a man in his late-30s asked me if I was a scout. I, of course, responded that I was with the San Francisco Giants. I was wearing a Giants hat (backwards, no less), so I didn't have much of a choice there. Sure, I travel with a big scorebook and seem knowledgeable when people talk to me, but does a writer sit in the stands with the average customer? Does a scout stand along side the wall of a park with other fans in an attempt to pick up autographs? How witless are these people?

Discontinuing the conversation with William was a treat, though I did feel sort of bad when I left because I had lied so much. When I looked at the bill and its added insurance charges, I cursed William and his list of questions which had caused me to take my eye off the ball. Apparently this was a very rare PT Cruiser since I was paying an additional hundred dollars for insurance. My thought was that the car was more delicate than a 14th century vase in an earthquake zone on the day when a kindergarten class visits a museum. Whatever; I was in Phoenix and ready for the Arizona Fall League.

Skipping check-in at the hotel, I immediately drove to Mesa in hopes of catching the final innings of the afternoon game between Peoria and Mesa, but arrived about 10 minutes late. I parked in the players' parking lot and looked around the stadium since this would be my only chance in Mesa. A few of the fall leaguers sauntered out of the clubhouse and were unsuccessful in dodging the autograph hunters (one of whom I had met before who bore a striking resemblance to boxing historian Bert Sugar, or at least his penchant for cigar smoking). I only stayed for 20 minutes, uneasy about parking illegally and just tramping around the park while workers were trying to clean. A 45-minute rush-hour traffic drive to the Super 8 Motel pretty much concluded my active day. I scampered across the street to a convenience store and bought some microwavable soup and a bag of Tostitos.

Sitting at the table in a Super 8 Motel with the fan blasting cold air into the room, I was scarfing down tomato soup (without a spoon) and chips at a furious pace. Stacks of unread Sports Illustrated sat on the table along with my scorebook, loose-leaf paper, car keys, and a Pittsburgh Pirates hat. The soup dripped from my lips every time I shoved a chip in my mouth as I scooped up the thin tomato paste. In between bites, I just couldn't help but repeat the same three words, over and over again.

"This is great," I said aloud to nothing but a flickering television.

It really is sad what two months without a live baseball game does to my life's overall standards.

Ersatz Liz

If the Halloween holiday occurred during the regular season, I can't imagine the fun the minor league franchises would have with it. The pageantry for such a holiday would certainly rival, if not surpass, that of the Fourth of July with its flag-waving and fireworks, which have become cheapened since half of the minor league teams set off fireworks once each home weekend. Most teams already forcefully promote some sort of "Halloween" day at the ballpark with workers dressing up and handing out candy to kids who have also come to the park in costume. However, when you are in Arizona and the normal rustling of dried, fallen leaves is silent in your ears and the crisp autumn aromas are absent from your nose, it just doesn't feel like Halloween, a lot like those doctored "Halloween" days at the park seem contrived and artificial. So it pleased me that the afternoon game at Phoenix Municipal Park made no attempts at reminding the fans that Tuesday, October 31st was Halloween. The fans themselves could remind me that freaks, in costume or not, are scattered across the country.

The Arizona Fall League is both half-ass and business-like in its operation. There is no set time that tickets go on sale (the theory is one hour prior to the game, but I purchased my ticket well outside of that time frame) and doors are open for anyone to walk in when they feel like it, though the fans are all courteous enough to wait for the gates to officially open an hour prior to the first pitch. During the first game I attended, the National Anthem was played without notice five minutes before one o'clock as players from both teams ran around in the outfield getting loose and grounds crew members continued to line the field, stopping quickly to remove their hats and put down their chalking devices to honor America for a minute and 15 seconds. The games move fairly quickly, despite the offensive outbursts that come from the warm climate and substandard pitching. With no introductory music for every player, no between inning contests or promotions, the game reverts back to its simplistic formula of being the entertainment.

Perhaps that no-frills attitude is what keeps fans from attending the games in Arizona. As one fan reminded me, the Arizona Fall League is one of the best-kept secrets in baseball. One hundred fifty-four people were counted in attendance on Tuesday afternoon. I'm not sure if that included the 40 scouts sitting behind home plate, but nevertheless, the stadium was emptier than Lynx Stadium in Ottawa during the month of April. Without unused season-tickets to distort the count for every game, there are no doctored attendance figures, making the one ticket-taker the official counter.

Directly behind home plate sat one-third of the populace, most holding radar guns and stopwatches. I am not particularly adept at picking out players from the past, especially when they have been hidden from my mind's eye for two decades, but I was told that numerous former players were charting the progress of the game's future on this afternoon. Ken Griffey, Ben Oglive, Pete Vuckovich, Ed Lynch, Billy Sample and Bill Mueller all wore sunglasses or hats to obscure their faces from the crowd. White Sox general manager Kenny Williams also sashayed his way through the scouts, shaking hands and smiling at old friends. After a few innings, I decided to drop in on Mr. Williams and a pair of scouts, hoping to eavesdrop on what they might have to say about some of the top prospects in front of them. I was disappointed when I plopped down two rows and a few seats over from the great baseball minds, hearing only the occasional remark about their golf games and family matters. It was equally frustrating to have them leave an inning later after my intrusion. I couldn't blame them. The Arizona Fall League season was already a couple of weeks old and they probably had seen whatever they needed to see from their prospects and a handful of others, and besides that, why would they want to share any secrets with another organization, no matter how friendly they might be with an opposing scout? The least Williams could have done was go off on Frank Thomas one more time. We were, after all, sitting at the Oakland A's spring training site, and Thomas was only a month removed from an MVP-type season less than a year after Williams berated him in an impromptu interview.

Pitchers periodically warmed up down the third base line from the on-field bullpen. A popping sound blasted throughout the stadium as the baseball came to a sudden stop in the catcher's glove, then repeated itself a half second later through the empty ballpark. Absent fans in the stands and nothing but the ballpark and the distant mountains lingering as a backdrop in the outfield, I couldn't help but feel as though I was called to this ballpark by special invitation. Just me and 150 strangers lucky enough to sit down quietly at a spring training site to watch some of the best young players in the country polishing up their craft.

Not that there was complete silence for two and a half hours. During the fourth or fifth inning, I noticed that a lone woman was clapping, for no particular player, during every at bat, whether the play resulted in a hit or an out. I appreciated her enthusiasm, but found it misguided, especially since no one else in the park was making a sound, save for the clicking of stopwatches by the scouts and the peeping of small birds flying from a support beam to the backstop wire. There was nothing wrong with her clapping; I actually found it a welcome change from the utter silence. Two other fans, with whom I had some discussions in the previous innings, filled me in on the woman.

"Are you going to the other game tonight in Scottsdale?" the older gentleman, wearing what looked like an Oneonta Tigers hat, asked.

"Yeah," I said.

"Just wait until tonight," the other fan said, a man in his late-30s with a shaved head. I later found he was from New Jersey and was visiting relatives. The other gentleman, probably around the age of 60, was originally from around Old Forge, NY, and then later moved to southern Connecticut, but now found himself living an hour north of Phoenix, a season-ticket holder of the Arizona Fall League. "Lucky bastard," I thought. He was able to see 50 or 60 games in the matter of weeks with minimal travel. After the conclusion of the Arizona trip, I would have traveled nearly 20,000 miles over the course of 225 days to see 57 games. Clearly, I am cursed by geography.

"What happens tonight?" I asked, my mind back on track.

"Just wait," Jersey said.

"Okay, I guess I can wait, but this better be worth it."

Part of the beauty of the Arizona Fall League is the opportunities it presents. For players, it is a chance to hone their abilities against similarly skilled ballplayers. For player development officials, it provides an instant scouting combine to see those same players and how they have progressed, allowing for future projections in the Rule 5 Draft or through trades. For fans, it gives anyone with an open weekend a chance to see all six teams play in a matter of two or three days, thanks to its doubleheaders. After watching the Grand Canyon Rafters (complete with studs Neil Walker and Troy Tulowitzki, among others) play the Phoenix Devil Dogs* (equally loaded with Travis Buck, Jeff Niemann, and the mercurial Elijah Dukes) at Phoenix Municipal Stadium, I would be driving just a few miles up the road to Scottsdale Stadium, where the Scottsdale Scorpions would play host to the Peoria Javelinas.**

---

* *Phoenix also employed Detroit Tigers pitching prospect Virgil Vasquez, who entertained his teammates in Erie, PA. I got a chance to talk a little with Virgil, but since he was charting this afternoon, I didn't learn enough about him to understand why he was named as the answer to so many questions that followed with giddy laughter by his teammates during their mid-June impromptu interviews. However, there was a certain way in his demeanor that made him seem like a bit of a hell raiser. Hopefully, I'll get a chance to talk to him in the future and discover more about that puff piece.*

** *There are two Peoria teams, one named the* Javelinas *(the J sounds like an H) and the* Saguaros. Saguaros *is pronounced, I believe, sa-hwa-rose, with a bit of a roll of the tongue. I was corrected numerous times in my enunciations and was looked down upon by others for my inability to say the word correctly. I failed to hang my head in shame. I bet none of them could even comprehend the Northern NY/Canadian word* tuque.

Upon entering Scottsdale Stadium, I couldn't help but notice this ballpark had unforgiving outfield dimensions. While the 330-foot distance to right field was normal, the center field distance of 430 feet would rival the deepest center fields among major league ballparks. Its 360-foot left field distance wasn't fair to right-handed pull hitters, either.

Finishing up batting practice, the Peoria Javelinas made way for infield-outfield practice for the home Scottsdale team. Around the infield were prospects Ryan Braun, Kevin Frandsen, Travis Ishikawa, Mark Reynolds, Matt Brown, Andy Gonzalez and Danny Richar, while roaming the outfield were Fred Lewis, Jerry Owens, Steve Moss, David Cook and Bradley Coon. The coaching staff rifled fungoes from all angles, giving a crisp fielding practice to tighten up the players' reflexes before game time. It is very rare for any fans to get inside a stadium to watch a true infield-outfield practice at the professional level, since most gates don't open until batting practice is completed and all the players have returned to grab a pre-game meal and change into their game uniforms. It is equally rare to hear someone bellowing at the top of their lungs in an empty stadium, cheering at every caught groundball and every throw across the diamond during a pre-game infield-outfield practice. Especially when that bellow is coming from a female.

The lone woman who sat two rows behind the dugout at Phoenix Municipal Stadium was in a similar position, this time on the first base side at Scottsdale Stadium, standing and clapping away. The woman, probably somewhere around 55 or 60 years of age, had a feathered coiffure of blonde hair just past the shoulders and strong facial features that reminded me of Liz Sheridan, the actress who played Jerry Seinfeld's mother on his sitcom in the 1990s. Every time someone did something positive, I expected her to turn to another fan in the crowd and say, "How could anyone not like him?" or if it was a negative play, just turn and frown with, "You were making out during Schindler's List?" Alas, it never happened.

"Great throw, Jerry," she shouted to centerfielder Jerry Owens as he short-hopped the cut between second base and the pitching mound. "Outstanding, Jerry. Best yet!" Owens trotted in from center field with his outfield throws complete, head down as to not make eye contact. Now the infielders were the centerpiece of her attention. Arizona Diamondbacks' prospect Mark Reynolds picked up a tough in-between hop at first base and fired the ball to second base, mimicking a 3-6-3 double play. "Outstanding, Mark! Great throw, great throw!"

"Why is she so much more...," I paused looking for the right word to ask my friend from Old Forge, "...animated here?"

"This is her home team," Old Forge replied.

"Her home team?" I questioned.

"Well, yes. She is an Arizona Diamondbacks season-ticket holder, and since this is where the Arizona prospects play, she cheers for this team, especially the Diamondbacks' prospects."

"She has enough money to be an Arizona season ticket holder?" I asked, glancing over at the questionably attired woman that could have forced this outfit together by rolling together spare change and whisking herself down to a thrift store.

"We're not really sure how she got her money," Old Forge continued. "We think that she married into it, maybe hooking up with a rock star back in the 70s, as a barfly."

"Great throw, Travis. Outstanding, big man, outstanding," she continued. Big first baseman Travis Ishikawa flashed a broad grin underneath the safety of the brim of his cap, trying not to laugh out loud at her antics. Even several weeks into the Arizona Fall League season, clearly this routine had not grown old. Old Forge had provided me with some valuable information and I thought of going over to the bogus Mrs. Seinfeld (who will now be known as BMS for short), to discover her story, but I didn't know where to begin. How do you approach a woman twice your age, sit down next to her and ask, "Wow, you sure are a lunatic...want to tell me the story of your life and how you got to be so crazy?" Instead, I decided to sit in the front row behind the dugout on the third base side, directly across from her, so I could take notes.

The Arizona night was growing cold. During the day, the temperature approached the mid-80s and, with no humidity, the afternoon was incredibly comfortable. Once the sun receded beyond the mountains, however, the heat disappeared and it dipped into the 50s. Unprepared in shorts and a t-shirt, I shivered through 11 innings of fall league baseball with only the occasional reprieve coming from the insulated bathrooms in the concourse.

Besides the entertainment on the field, BMS was putting on a show of her own to keep me warm. Her undulating and rocking in her seat dwarfed the movements of major league pitching coach Leo Mazzone, making him appear almost stagnant in comparison. Along with the variety of actions BMS performed in her seat, her pre-game mid-range voice dropped to an alto and bordered on a male's bass. She also became the queen of positive reinforcement, despite the nonsensical actions on the field. With the bases loaded and one out, Mark Reynolds fielded a one-hopper to first base, touched the bag and then wheeled towards second to throw out the now unforced runner, who instinctively decided to turn back towards first—and let the runner score from third—before being tagged out on the double play. The run counted since the force was negated once Reynolds touched first base, and he understood his folly as he jogged back to the dugout with slumped shoulders and a disappointed look upon his face. It mattered little to BMS, who cheered pitcher Manny Parra for getting the groundball he needed to get out of the inning. "*Great* job, *Man-nee! Way* to *go!*"

That was the truly terrific part of her cheering. Her staccato speech allowed her to put emphasis on nearly every single syllable she spoke. "*Out-stand-ing, Jer-ree!* Best, yet, *Jer-ree!*" Her head nodded forward violently with each word, its forcefulness seeming to take otherworldly effort and its ferocity matched only by the rapid recoil as her neck muscles sent the skull back to its normal spot on the spine. Though I'm sure she mastered this approach after years of head banging in her supposed rock star, groupie days, I couldn't help but feel concerned for her. With white knuckles, she grasped a metal bar that attached to the dugout and her thrusts were coming dangerously close to a collision between steel and bone.

"*Come on, Mark, let* it be *yours!*" she shouted to Mark Reynolds in his next at bat. "Great choice, great *choice*, come on, Mark, base *hit!*" she repeated as he let two knee-high fastballs go by on the inside corner. She almost appeared woozy when hollering the word *hit*, as if she suffered a head rush. When Reynolds came through with a hit, the feeling left her as she leapt to her feet in joy and gushed, "*Out-stand-ing!*"

After she congratulated Jaime D'Antona for warming up the pitcher in between innings, I had heard enough. It was one thing to cheer impressive outfield throws and the fine picks of an infield practice, but to stand and applaud for the backup catcher to kneel behind home plate and catch a few warm up tosses from the pitcher was beyond reason, so my eyes began to wander.

It was late in the game, when I noticed an oddity in my favorite place, the bullpen. I've seen some amazing things in the bullpen this year, and while what I thought to be a pornographic blow up doll in the home bullpen at Tri-City was an interesting addition, the game of "William Tell" that I witnessed in Arizona takes top prize. To fight off boredom, the players were taking turns throwing a baseball at another player from about 50 feet away. One player would put on a catcher's mask and place a paper cup on the top of his head. The pitchers would then throw baseballs in an attempt to knock the paper cup off the "catcher's" head cleanly without hitting him in the face. Sometimes the pitchers were successful and other times not, but every one of them appeared to be enjoying themselves. I'm not sure if this was an original idea or if it was a version of what happened an inning earlier when one of the fans on the first base side attempted to catch an arching foul pop with his hat that missed his chapeau and landed squarely upon the top of his head, bounding into the next set of seats. Peoria's Jacoby Ellsbury, leaning on the rail of the dugout, turned and mouthed "Oooh," to his teammates while Kevin Kouzmanoff, who was in the on-deck circle at the time, came back and laughed a bit to his teammates, saying, "Shit. Get up and get out of the way, or something." The older fan returned a few outs later with an ice bag placed on his head, mostly unharmed.

The game started out with robust offense due to awful pitching from the starters Manny Parra and Bobby Livingston as the teams matched four-run first innings. I would like to say the game seesawed back and forth, but it really was just ineffective pitching, and it bothered me as both pitchers struggled to control the strike zone and command their pitches. Eventually, the Scottsdale pitchers settled down and struck out 15 hitters through the first nine innings, but the game went into extras and my hands were becoming too numb to keep score. If I, a northerner, found this cold, I could only imagine what the locals thought of such weather. I was the only idiot wearing shorts, though.

A couple of near misses in extra innings prolonged the game to the bottom of the 11th, which would be the final inning due to league rules. Major league teams try to shorten AFL games during the non-traditional season as to not cause any unnecessary wear on the pitchers' arms, even though the majority of these pitchers were generally not considered the cream of the prospect crop. Regardless, the Scorpions did not force a suspended game by being inept in the 11th as Ryan Braun led off with a double and then scored on a base hit from Mark Reynolds.

As Braun slid through home plate with the game-winning run, I envisioned BMS hopping the dugout rail and making her way towards Reynolds while morphing into Morganna the Kissing Bandit. I was disappointed as I watched her exuberantly jump up and down with ever increasing enthusiasm, her voice up an octave as she cheered. With the game no longer hanging in the balance, her intensity vanished and her love of the game and her team returned to a childlike form. It was easy for everyone to mock her voice, her attire, her incessant clapping and her incredibly strong neck muscles, but was it really necessary? While she may have disturbed the otherwise quiet crowd, BMS was constantly positive, even consoling in her tone when mistakes occurred, and her devotion to a less-than-a-decade-old franchise is unbelievable. She goes to *Arizona Fall League* games to see a glimpse of the future. Five years from now, she may not even remember Ryan Braun as a member of the Scottsdale Scorpions, but I bet she recalls the kid who came up to pinch-hit for Randy Johnson in September 2002 who was only sipping from the major league proverbial cup of coffee. It's just another way of being a fan, and as obnoxious as she was, I think everyone at one time or another would like to say they held a team that close to their heart.

As long as that team isn't the Yankees.

Epilogue—
Wait Until Next Year!

A few times since I began regularly visiting minor league stadiums four years ago, I've crossed paths with fans that were brazenly trying to visit every minor league ballpark in a single summer. I'm unaware whether or not those nomads ever accomplished their goals. I was first alerted about one of these bold vagabonds in 2003 when I was at a Carolina Mudcats game, along with a few hundred other fans on a dismal May evening in Zebulon, North Carolina. An usher and I became engaged in conversation and I told her that I was traveling around the south to visit different ballparks. She asked if I was "the guy." I didn't think there was any advance notice for me, so I concluded that I was not "the guy" to whom she was referring. "The guy" was some American traveler who was attempting to make his way to every minor league ballpark in one summer. It baffled me that anyone would want to even try to complete such a mission. How could anyone possibly enjoy himself knowing that every morning (if you were lucky enough to sleep) you would have to pry yourself out of bed and drive several hours to the next event? When do you find time to accomplish regular tasks like laundry, dishes, bathing, exercise or anything resembling leisure? Where do you get the money for gas, hotels, or plane fare, let alone the $1,000 in tickets before you even take a bite to eat in a six-month trip?

In 2006, with support from I know not where, documentary filmmaker Cass Sapir completed the goal and visited every major and non-independent minor league ballpark in the United States. His goal was to not only see every single park, but to raise money for the Jimmy Fund (his supporter?), a charity for cancer research that has raised over 400 million dollars since its inception nearly 60 years ago. Obviously, Sapir had a higher calling in mind with his trip than the excursions I've made over the past four summers. I certainly cannot fault anyone who is trying to raise money through donations and a post-season online auction. I do, however, wonder if his sacrifice was as great as mine. Sure, he drove three times as many miles as I did and crisscrossed the country on numerous occasions to suit the demanding schedule makers, but I have a feeling his budget was considerably greater than the one for which I scrimped and saved. He was featured in an October edition of *Baseball America*, chronicling his 175-day trip. Though I, too, received media attention for my summer trip, it was on a much more modest scale: a Sunday newspaper puff piece basically advertising the as-of-that-time *unfinished* book you have nearly completed.

The above may sound like envy, but it's not a matter of jealousy towards anyone who tries to accomplish the feat of seeing every park during one summer. I can't comprehend why anyone would try it. It's the equivalent of sitting down at a fine restaurant and ordering everything on the menu in one visit and shoveling all of it down your throat in 30 minutes. Baseball, like a fine meal, should be savored, allowing your senses to enjoy every portion.

With all of that understood, anyone who knows me would probably believe that I was under great duress when the next sentence is written. I'm tired of going to baseball games. The games themselves will always entertain me and my adoration for the game is something that I cannot even quantify, but the preparation, the financial strain, the time spent driving from ballpark to ballpark drains me both mentally and physically. It's exactly why I can't imagine why anyone would forcibly send himself or herself back and forth across the country just to say they saw every park in one summer.

It's difficult to ascertain how much effort is expended into my, or someone like Cass Sapir's, baseball endeavors. As the major league pennant races draw to a close and football is beginning to take over the attention of the sporting crowd, I have, for the past three years, immediately begun to check every minor league baseball website for new scheduling information for the following season, formulating yet another summer's worth of excursions. Hundreds of hours are spent searching the schedules of every team in the country and then the lists are systematically entered into several mazes of logic that can only be understood by me without some moderate hand-held interpretation. As soon as game times are finalized and released to the public, small trips are considered. Then reservations are made with friends of mine who have no idea what their personal plans will entail on some random Tuesday in the middle of August several months before spring has even arrived. It's not fair to my friends, but they all understand my idiosyncrasies and pacify me with all the answers I want to hear, only to change their minds at the most inopportune times.

All of these things sometimes force me to contemplate quitting my sojourns, as I wonder if there is some kind of baseball version of a nicotine patch to cut the cravings. Traveling from game to game is wearing me down. I feel as if the games and the preparation define me as a person. It's one of the few things that acquaintances ask me about. Hell, it's one of the few things that my closest friends ask me about. I used to ridicule people who could discuss nothing but their jobs or their families. I thought that those people were out of touch with reality, living a life inside of the walls of what they could touch without breaking through to imagine anything immediately outside of their own five senses. It was pathetic to me. Now it appears to others that I've become just that which I loathe: someone who can only grasp a single subject and is lost without it as a crutch.

While driving in August, I couldn't help but think that my baseball travels mimic my life in a sort of metaphoric way, which bothers me to no end because I despise the academic bores who analyze everything to death. The traveling for baseball games could mirror my desire for the open, free and detached life I lead, allowing me to do whatever I like, whenever I like. However, now that I've grown tired of all of the traveling, perhaps that symbolizes a need to settle down and get my life in order with some semblance of normalcy.

Then again, the parable could be that the travel has allowed me to push forth personal growth that wasn't present prior to all my movements across the country, and that I'm not weary, but feel drained because the growth has completed and I'm continuing on a journey that is unnecessary, much the way the first marathon runner could have stopped and let someone else carry on his news, but instead pushed on to proclaim his battle report before collapsing in death. The importance is certainly not the same, but the overzealous pushing is similar. I can't imagine that anyone would ever think that they have no further room for growth as a person, but maybe this part of my growth is finished and my inner self realizes there are other items on which to work.

Just a few miles after coming to my, albeit odd, epiphany, I drove past a tree that was felled by a violent thunderstorm. Amazingly, this happened to be the same sturdy tree that brought my jeep to a sudden and complete stop more than three years earlier when an icy road forced me into its steadfast path (I always claimed I didn't run into the tree, but the tree ran out in front of me in the road) at 50 miles per hour. Somehow I survived the collision without much damage, just a couple of deep bone bruises on my shins where I cracked the plastic under-portion of the dashboard and another minor bruise on my chest where the seatbelt held me. The tree was cracked by the recent storm, but I had easily survived the storm, in fact mocked its severity when others were concerned the previous night. Sudden elation returned to me, and I thought that there was no reason to ever stop traveling to games, that I was in some way immortal because I survived the storm and this immovable piece of nature was snapped like a twig. It was then that I felt my shins to feel the inch-long scar and dent in my right leg, which seemed like it would never heal back in 2003. Instead of continued elation, I returned my hands to their accustomed spots on the steering wheel, understanding luck, timing, and perhaps divine intervention make for a long life rather than some misconceived notion of an everlasting corporeal body.

Clearly there is no immortality and no one can be assured of the future. It's something I've always adored about baseball. It's safe to say that no two baseball games have ever gone the same, as the potential outcomes are so endless. Yet with so many possibilities in so many seasons, games, innings, at bats and pitches, players can often recall the exact sequence of events without missing a beat. It's remarkable. So is the game.

And that is why I'll be back at the ballparks again next year and for every year after that. You don't know what lies ahead and why wouldn't you want to enjoy every moment of your life, even if you have to endure seven-hour drives in each direction in the same day? Maybe you will get to see an unassisted triple play or a perfect game that day and I like my chances against another tree jumping out in front of me. Baseball and life are worth the gamble.

Printed in the United States
82768LV00002B/112/A